Y0-BQY-075

MILLER, RUSSELL R.

SNAPSHOTS: A BRIEF STROLL THROUGH ASIA

338.95

GIFT: RUSSELL R. MILLER

NF

1/17/2014

Also by Russell R. Miller

An American in Shanghai: Reflections on Living in New China
East Wind Press, San Francisco, CA 2013

Spring: Engaging Nature's Renewal in Rural Japan
Lulu Enterprises Inc., Morrisville, NC 2007

Singapore's Homegrown Entrepreneurs Tell You How to Do It
Landmark Books Pte. Ltd., Singapore 2003

Impressions
Arion Press, San Francisco, CA 1991

Supergrowth: Buying and Selling Agencies for Profit
The National Underwriter Company, Cincinnati, OH 1981

Photographs by Russell R. Miller

Gateway to World Religions
AsiaPac Books Pte. Ltd., Singapore 2007

My Singapore Story: My Heritage, My Dream
AsiaPac Books Pte. Ltd., Singapore 2005

Snapshots
A Brief Stroll Through Asia

Russell R. Miller

for my fellow PLC members

Dec 13

East Wind Press
SHANGHAI • SAN FRANCISCO

Back cover photograph copyright © 2013 Russell R. Miller
Project Manager: Peter Beren, PETERBEREN.COM
Book design by Mark Shepard SHEPGRAPHICS.COM
Edited by Peter Beren

Miller, Russell R., 1937-
    Snapshots : a brief stroll through Asia / by Russell
R. Miller. — First edition.
    pages cm
    ISBN 978-0-9911354-5-5 (hc)
    ISBN 978-0-9911354-6-2 (pbk.)
    ISBN 978-0-9911354-7-9 (ebook)

    1. Economic development—Asia—Anecdotes. 2. Asia—
Economic conditions—Anecdotes. 3. Investment banking—
Asia—Anecdotes. 4. Miller, Russell R., 1937-
5. Investment bankers—Biography.   I. Title.

HD82.M55 2013   338.95
                         QBI13-600195

First Edition

To those who supported our business and charitable efforts as we explored our way through the underbrush, eventually revealing the ennobling joys of unknown people and places.

Hanoi, Vietnam. Hoàn Kiếm Lake.

Contents

Shanghai, China. Shanghai International
Business and Economics University.

Maps

Shanghai, China.

Introduction

This is not a travelogue or a diary of visits and adventures in Asia. If I could write as well as Somerset Maugham when he sketched his vivid impressions in *On a Chinese Screen*, I would do it. What follows are recollections of memorable moments and vivid people I have met in countries ranging from Japan to Indonesia. I have lived in some of these places, and others I just briefly passed through, but all have touched me in some deep way.

Share the saunter, meet the people. It will change you.

Shanghai, Datian Lu, 2013

Hong Kong.

Hong Kong

When Ulysses S. Grant stepped off his ship in Hong Kong Harbor, it was John Pope Hennessy, the governor, who welcomed him. Over time and during too many visits to count, I gradually have fallen out of love with what one of my shirttail cousins, James Pope Hennessy, called Half-Crown Colony in his book on Hong Kong. His grandfather, who was also my Dad's great-uncle, was the eighth governor of Hong Kong, from 1877 to 1883. He subsequently fell out with the foreign office and was exiled to become governor of Mauritius, a small island nation off the coast of Africa. He loved it there, and so did I when I visited on behalf of the nonprofit Spirit of Enterprise, which I had begun in Singapore in 2002 and had subsequently spread to Mauritius.

There I continued to cross paths, figuratively, with "uncle" John Pope Hennessy. One day I found myself addressing the entire business elite of Mauritius in one of those two-story colonial government houses along the mall that faces Parliament. As I was giving my speech I glanced out the window and there below me, facing the Parliament, was none other than Governor John Pope Hennessy in the afternoon light atop his pedestal. Ironic how one's history can come around full circle.

Even more ironic is the odd fact that his grandson, James, sat in our Nevada home facing Lake Tahoe and typed away, updating his obituary of Edward VIII, who by secret telegram the *London Times* had alerted James that the former king was on his deathbed and the obit needed updating. It was so incongruous, seeing this famous writer typing away for the *Times* well before the good citizens of England knew what was happening. There, of course, was no Internet so all the transmissions were done by Western Union, which then retyped the text and at the other end pasted long strips of the typing on their transmittal sheets to be hand delivered.

I once mentioned to my good client Simon Keswick, who was reigning "Taipan of the Noble House" (Jardines), that my great-uncle had arrested and thrown his grandfather in jail. "Yes," he said, "and did you know he was a queer?" I didn't know that, but it didn't surprise me at all because I knew both his grandsons were gay.

I'd already witnessed Hong Kong's history looping back on itself. When I first arrived, I worked with the slowly withdrawing Jardine Matheson, once one of Hong Kong's original and most venerable trading houses. I saw the Hong Kong Club fade in importance as the China Club gained prominence, and I was there to celebrate Handover in 1997.

In the early days, when I was still new to Hong Kong, I used to thrill at landing in the old Kai Tak airport. You swooped between the city's tall buildings, so close that you hoped the plane wouldn't catch someone's laundry and whisk it away, snagged on the wing.

For a while I had an office in the tallest tower in Hong Kong, Wan Chai's Central Tower, and used to stay at the old Ritz Carleton, which was shoehorned into a skinny building on the harbor.

As impressive as these towers were and still are, I've always felt the scale of the buildings in Hong Kong, and how they relate to the pedestrians, was out of kilter. The many walkways only reinforce this diminished feeling. You have to get to the Cenotaph and City Hall, with its old government buildings, to get any feeling that you are in harmony with your surroundings.

One way to be in harmony with your fellow man, or at least, your fellow man who liked to drink, was to go to the rugby Sevens at Hong Kong Stadium. Ostensibly this is a rugby competition, but in reality it is a huge, drunken, outrageous few days of pure levity and unending business entertainment. Companies reserved suites and filled them with a cornucopia of food and drink. People would dress in costumes, which got crazier in the stands further away from the snazzy suites. Trying to get the most out of the event, you picked the host you wanted to spend some time with, and then ate or drank to your heart's content. Of course you tried to hit as many of the parties as possible, all the while casting an occasional glance at the Kiwi or Fiji Islanders attempting to kill each other on the rugby pitch.

Once when I was sitting with Philip Tose, a founder of Peregrine Investment Holdings, in the midst of a large group of his very rowdy, very drunk traders, brokers and other employees, I mentioned their wild behavior. "Yes," he said. "That's why we hire them. We like their spirit." He then pointed to one of the tall towers not too far from the stadium, and told me he had just spent $10 million for two floors of it, and that his wife, a TaiTai as they called the ladies of society, would likely spend more than that decorating it. Unfortunately for him, as well as for all his exuberant employees, Peregrine shortly thereafter collapsed with the default of an Indonesian company ironically called "Steady Safe." Though it was neither steady nor safe, that company still exists today and is still running. Peregrine is not.

Peregrine managed an investment fund I had raised that dealt in insurance securities all over Asia. When they collapsed I had to assure my investors, which included Citibank and Marsh McLennan, that we were not in jeopardy. All our holdings were in separate companies not attached to Peregrine; they managed, but didn't actually hold, any of the securities. Nevertheless, when we were winding things up after the collapse, we had to deal with a huge international CPA firm that was appointed as Peregrine's trustee. It was a nightmare in the sense that they wanted to charge us the same exorbitant rates they were charging for the bankruptcy, and I had very huge fights with their allocated billing when in fact we were not a part of the actual bankruptcy. After several acrimonious meetings they finally gave in and settled on a set, fixed fee and made quick work of our papers, the outcome I had been advocating all along.

In the process, I learned a lot about places I had never heard of, like Labuan, a federal territory of East Malaysia off the coast of Sabah, where we had stored our Korean holdings because of a unique tax treaty. I also became familiar with the unique characteristics of the Irish Stock Exchange where our Ascendant Capital fund was listed.

We had holdings in seven countries. Of course you have to constantly visit them, and the brokers who handle your account won't let you pass through without some exotic dining.

This always led my colleagues and me to consume outrageously extravagant multi-course meals in various venues. The Korean meals were the most over-the-top in terms of multiple dishes, but the live shrimp dishes in Hong Kong vied as the most off-putting, as shrimp scuttled around each plate trying to avoid the ultimate spearing.

One quirky thing about Hong Kong today is that it can be used to fulfill a Chinese visa requirement to "leave China" from time to time for twenty-four hours. It's the difference between sovereignty and administration. Although the Chinese government selects the governor, they leave the actual running of Hong Kong mostly to the feisty citizens of Hong Kong.

I felt lucky to be in Hong Kong for the Handover. The day the last governor, Chris Patten, as arrogant as ever, left his official residence in his Rolls-Royce for the last time, I was with the crowd surrounding Government House. As the stately Rolls slowly eased out into the street, the crowd booed him, clapped for him, and sang "Auld Lang Syne" all at once—a cacophony of competing sounds accurately reflecting the tangle of the city's emotions.

Later that night, I stood on a blocked-off overpass in the rain and thought about the old saying, "The sun never sets on the British

Empire." It certainly seemed to set as the last notes from the bands faded; Patten and Prince Charles, the ever-waiting king in his white uniform, departed; their ship, the *Britannia*, lurched off the dock and headed into the night while Hong Kong partied into the morning "shaking the dust from their sandals" and making ready for the new dawn.

The *San Francisco Chronicle* reporter sent to cover the story asked what I thought of the Handover. "I think it is great," I told him. "That's not our story," he said, and abruptly ended the interview. That was the attitude of much of the western coverage. They wanted verification of how terrible it was going to be and how scared the population was, fearful of the march of the Chinese army coming across at midnight. What a disservice they did to their readers. Most people I knew agreed that this was a positive change. Yes, the over-exaggerated official Chinese line—"the end of a century of humiliation is over"—was a little over top, but when I returned to China itself the next day, I felt the genuine pride of the people, who were in consensus: China is back, the Brits are gone and we're glad to see their backs.

Macau

A few years ago I re-visited Macau after not having been there since the "post-Lisboa" casinos were built. In prior years the Lisboa was the only casino, and it was controlled by Stanley Ho Hung Sun, 何鴻燊, the legendary "King of Gambling." His hotel, the Lisboa, was connected to one of his main casinos and next to the convention center. It was the focus of much activity, including large infestations of ladies of dubious reputation!

In 1998 or so, I and two colleagues from Russell Miller Asia Advisors booked into the Lisboa, because it was the convention hotel for an international insurance conference. While dining in the coffee shop, I noticed a large number of ladies sitting at the counter, who were obviously not sitting there to have dinner. How can you tell they are not there to have dinner? Short hot pants, tight blouses and staring at anyone who entered the restaurant. I asked my Singapore office head to go ask the manager what was going on. A few minutes later he came back laughing and told us that it was the policy of the Lisboa to have lots of these women around "because that's what our casino customers like." The coffee shop was just the hors d'oeuvre, so to speak. There were ladies in the lobby, at the entrance, and even around the shops. They were the canapés lazing around for the gamblers and hotel guests to pick up.

The boldest thing I experienced was in an elevator on the way to my room. At an intermediate floor a lady got on who had obviously just finished a job, and she immediately offered to accompany me to my room. Now that's express service. I demurred!

Macau, China.
Cathedral ruins of
St. Paul in background.

My previous visits to Macau had all been focused on meeting with a group of Jesuit priests who had a church, offices and living quarters on Largo de Sto. Agostinho, in the old Portuguese quarter, with its lovely pastel painted buildings and colonial feel. Part of the street was taken up by the residence, and next to it was a typical-looking European-style Jesuit church. Down the block was a complex of buildings housing the headquarters of Caritas, the main office for their many charitable efforts.

During my convention visit I made time for lunch with the Jesuits, and they asked where I was staying. When I said the Lisboa, their response was sincere, "Oh Russell, we don't go there."

Years ago at the behest of my friend, the late Father Edward J. Malatesta, S.J., who was the founder of the University of San Francisco's Ricci Institute for Chinese-Western Cultural History,* urged me to go to Macao and meet the Spanish priest, Father Luis Ruiz Suarez, S.J., who was doing some remarkable work with lepers in China.

It's wonderful to meet a real saint. Fr. Ruiz, a rugged, gray-haired, stocky man, lived most of his 97 years in Macao and founded Caritas Macao, helping a variety of those in need there, and built a network that later helped sustain scores of leper colonies and homes for HIV/Aids children. He survived prison, being banned from China as a possible spy, rode his motor bike everywhere and was a fan of Real Madrid. Who wouldn't love him? The locals

---

*The center was named after the famous Jesuit Matteo Ricci, who arrived in Macao in 1582 and then lived in various cities throughout China. In 1601, Ricci was invited to become an advisor to the Imperial court of the Wanli Emperor, the first westerner to be invited into the Forbidden City. This honor was in recognition of Ricci's scientific abilities, chiefly his predictions of solar eclipses, which were significant events in the Chinese world. In Shanghai, in Xujiahui section of the city, there are statues of Ricci and Xu Guangqi conversing. Xu Guangqi was a very important Ming official, and is buried there in a lovely little park. One of my friend's grandfather's grandfather raised chrysanthemums in this very area in the 1800s. It now is one of the most busy and built-up shopping areas in Shanghai.

called him "Father of the Poor" and "Angel of Macao." He was that and more.**

Many a time I visited him at Casa Ricci, the Jesuit residence. One night I accepted the Jesuits' hospitality to stay all night in the residence. It was very humble and, unfortunately for me, in perfect keeping of their vow of poverty. The straw mattress kept me tossing and turning all night. The building was built to house more than thirty, and I think at the time I was there, it had five. My floor was sparsely inhabited.

Across the street was a large seminary building that had been closed some time before. Working their many activities, the Jesuits were aging fast and not being replenished in any numbers by younger men. What will happen to all the social services and the three schools they run when they disappear? Who will take their place?

Fr. Ruiz was totally focused on his poor. One time, after my establishing an endowment for the lepers, I visited him and expected some praise for what I had done. At least a pat on the back. Father said, "Russell, I don't like what you have done, making an endowment." Huh? "Father, it will last 1,000 years and generate income every single year." "No, no, they need help *now*." I was humbled by his focus on the poor he served. He was practical. That reminded me of Mother Teresa, who once when asked by the mayor of New York, in an expansive gesture, What could he do for her? she replied, "Give me a parking place in front of our convent."

Father Ruiz and Fr. Gregory took me to visit Tai Kam Island. This

---

**Father Ruiz worked with refugees, and founded the first housing in Macao specifically established to house the elderly. The Ricci Centre for Social Services evolved into Caritas Macau. Under Caritas, Fr. Ruiz opened five centers throughout Macao that provided services for the mentally disabled. During the 1980's, he began working with lepers in Guangdong Province with the help of an order of Catholic nuns, the Sisters of Charity of St. Anne. He first went to Tai Kam Island in 1986, where 200 lepers had been exiled.

is one of the many venues that the Chinese government used to deposit lepers to take them out of society. Leprosy is still seen in some quarters as a Biblical disease requiring removal and permanent quarantine. In fact it isn't even called leprosy in most of the world because of the stigma attached to the word. It is called Hansen's disease. The truth is that it is now completely curable before any harm comes to a person, but in China, at least for now, there just isn't enough knowledge, will or maybe even medical attention to get it eradicated. The government ended its policy of sending people to leper colonies in the mid-1980's, but either through ostracism in villages or self-exile, many colonies remain active.

Tai Kam is about forty miles from Macao off the coast of Guangdong. We took a little outboard motorboat and headed out into the South China Sea, passing fishing boats pulling up full nets, and aimed for the open sea. There was nothing there. After what seemed like forever, in the far horizon the outlines of an island emerged.

After we landed at the wooden pier we were greeted by some of the inhabitants. It is hard to describe the horror that goes through your mind when a leper holds his hand out in greeting. Of course you shake hands. It's a little like when you think the wing is falling off your airliner but you don't say anything for fear of making a fool of yourself.

Leprosy is a disease that, once it progresses, can make people quite repulsive, with digits and limbs missing, and faces disfigured. A group had gathered in the chapel for mass, displaying every possible disfigurement. It was hard to be with them at first. What was surprising to me is that as the day went on their disfigurement faded, and we began to see them as just regular people going about the business of life. They had wives and children and housing provided by the Jesuits, and wonderful nuns from India lived there with them. They had vegetable gardens, playgrounds and what you would expect of a very small community. They just were on an island in the middle of nowhere. The Chinese government provided a rice allotment and other help. During my visit I used a small sketchbook I carried around to do a picture of the area. While so doing, a young boy named Gam watched me and then asked if I would include him in the drawing. I did.

Fr. Gregory told me an amusing story. He said that every once in a while the local government official in charge of the area would steal the little boat that was used to transport people and goods to and from the island. This was the same kind of a boat we were using. Fr. Gregory said that the official would periodically gamble and, of course, lose. The official would then arrange the theft of their boat and sell it to meet some debts. When I asked Fr. Gregory did he mind, his reply was, "That's just doing business in China."

He did however tell me about the time the very same official shorted the rice allotment. Three sisters, not one over five feet tall, got in the boat, went to his office and, as Fr. Gregory tells it, well, he didn't know what they said, but whatever it was, the official is still trembling. He never shorted the rice again!

When we were getting ready to leave in the late afternoon, a small group had gathered on the pier to see us off. Fr. Gregory said that they wanted to say something to me in thanks for the help I had given. They gathered around me. Here was a group, tall and short, often shirtless, in some cases toothless, some disfigured, and they started to sing a Texas cowboy song in Chinese, "The Red River Valley." I have never been so touched, nor have any idea how they learned it. Tears flowed all around.

A friend of mine in the TV documentary field, at my request, agreed to do a program showing the work of Fr. Ruiz and the others in China. I arranged the financing, and the idea was to use the program to raise funds. Fr. Ruiz demurred, he said something along the lines of "Russell, it might make the Chinese government mad to expose their problems. Just leave it alone. We will raise funds somehow."

He knew well that the government sometimes acted without a lot of information, even, bizarrely, barring him as a spy for a while. It was so ridiculous a charge that they later removed the ban. At that time, of course, Macau was still Portuguese and you had to get a visa to get into China even though Macau is literally across the street.

Although I've already mentioned some of his accomplishments, let me finish up by recounting a few more things this humble man did. According to the people at Caritas, he looked after more than eight thousand patients in 139 centers, helped the families and children of the lepers with building some fifteen roads, seventeen schools, and five bridges; manning and operating seven mobile clinics; installing twenty-five systems for clean drinking water and twenty-one systems for electricity; all the while showing incredible love for all the afflicted.

I last saw him in 2011, his body gnarled by age, finally confined to a wheelchair but with his spirit vibrant and electric. As our visit finished I asked for his blessing and knelt in front of his wheelchair. He whispered a brief prayer and raised his right arm as Xavier had, and blessed me. He received greetings in heaven a few months later.

Taiwan

Drinking snake blood isn't the most intuitively desirous thing to do. I was led to Snake Alley as a "must see" of Taipei. All along the alley are various stands selling snake meat and blood. I forget what snake blood is supposed to do, but I downed a small shot glassful. It was awful. I didn't find it made my hair grow, enhance my libido, improve my eyesight or stand up straight.

When I was trying to buy an insurance company for my fund, Ascendant Capital, I spent many a day at the offices of China Mariners' Assurance Corp. (台湾中国航联产物保险) an old-line company that had been started in China and in 1949 moved to Taiwan. It still had on its books mainland shareholders, although a Taiwan family through an operating company controlled it. I thought it would be great to reintroduce it into China, although in the late 1990's it wasn't possible to get permission from either government. However, that's not how things actually worked. One of the leading owners of a Taiwan company had told me he had set up several branches of his listed company in mainland China. "How do you do it?" "We tell them we are selling noodles." Obviously not the whole story but you get the drift.

China Mariners also had a pretty good experience writing business over many years, and was one of the few companies that weren't starved for capital. Of the top twenty companies, about two-thirds were broke from a technical-analysis point of view. The Taiwan regulatory authorities recognized this, but like the Japanese regulators and many others they were not willing to close down some of their largest financial companies. They let them run with overvalued assets that for the most part were illusionary, but provided "cover" for letting them continue, until the regulators could work something out. This they did over the ensuing years by pushing the more feeble companies into those that could at least stand on their own.

The leading family of China Mariners eventually sold the business to another Taiwan company. I was not surprised it happened, although the reported price paid was way beyond what we had projected a few years before. This is an illustration of how difficult it is to get the real story out of a local company if you aren't from that country, and doubly hard to complete a transaction without being a national insider. Sure, the companies that are in dire straits are available, but no sane person would buy them.

As outsiders, we faced this difficulty time after time. Many of the companies that were offered to us were the national subsidiaries of a British or American company that had decided to abandon a country. They then tried to sell off their local entity. This strategy usually was not successful, as the potential buyers didn't have the same international rating as the parent companies of these subsidiaries, and so the result of a sale would be that after a change in ownership many of the customers would move their business to another international company. The other difficulty was that fully operating companies in a country had all the staff in place and the experience to fold into their existing operations. The costs and efficiency of this often trumped our offers, and at the end of the day, the locals always had an advantage.

You always had to be very careful in your analysis. One life insurance company we looked at had policies on its books that paid guaranteed interest for the policy life that was linked to the last survivor of the household. Needless to say the projections went decades out and when you calculated the ability of the insurance company to meet these obligations, it was impossible. They were technically broke. The regulators just pretended the company could meet their future obligations and scurried around to find a greater fool. We weren't it.

A similar situation arose with a Hong Kong company we had been offered for USD $60 million. It had business in about five countries in Asia, and we were very interested. By the time we were finished analyzing it our offer was: "Give us USD $10 million and we will take it off your hands." This outraged the management, and they stormed out of our final meeting claiming we were completely off in our calculations. The CEO was especially incensed since over many years he had put this amalgamation of companies together. Within about a year they were insolvent, forcibly taken over by the authorities and folded into another company. To add an element of intrigue, the CEO was killed in an accident as he was riding his motorcycle to work, just before a very pivotal meeting. Rumors of murder immediately surfaced, with suspicions that some of his more shadowy activities that might have come to light were now squelched. It was never resolved and just floated, like many rumors, into the back alleys of Hong Kong.

When I was introduced to Taiwan insurance companies, my first meeting turned out to be quite remarkable. I was asked to a private luncheon with the head of the insurance association. He was a retired general and was extremely well connected in the small circle of power brokers. To my astonishment, when I arrived at his office lunch was going to be there in one of the conference rooms, and in it awaited the CEOs of every major Taiwanese insurance company. It was quite an introduction.

Later that very evening I was having dinner with yet another insurance executive, and the general walked into the restaurant and greeted me as he passed our table. My dinner companions were amazed. "How do you know him, etc., etc.?" My prestige zoomed, at least for those few minutes. Of course, I couldn't have planned such a fortuitous meeting if I had tried, because I had been in Taiwan exactly one day.

One of the logistical difficulties of trying to buy a company in Taiwan was their very strict visa requirements for Chinese passport holders. Several of my best employees were mainland Chinese, and when I wanted to bring them to Taiwan the bureaucratic paperwork was voluminous. Among other things, we had to have a written letter of invitation from a Taiwan company asking us to visit. They had to affirm various things about us that I forget, but basically, it was that we were going to do what we said we were there for. In addition, we had to give an hour-by-hour schedule for every day we planned to stay. This especially irritated me, since much of what an investment group does we keep very secret, for fear a competitor will discover our targets and go after them. Who knows where all this paperwork ended up, but, reluctantly, visas were always issued. Today, of course, much of that has been done away with on both sides of the straits.

Early in the 1980's I had flown into Taipei for one day just to do a little sightseeing. Obviously, America and Taiwan were very close friends, and it never occurred to me that I might need a visa. I arrived about five in the evening and was going to just look around and leave the next day fairly early. "Where is your visa?" "I don't have one. Do I need it?" "Please sit over there and we will get back to you." Hours later an officer said I couldn't come into Taiwan and that they were confiscating my passport until I was scheduled to leave the next day. I would have to stay in their approved hotel not too far from the airport and would be driven there. Ok, and off we went. The hotel was paid for, I think by them, and after seeing me registered and telling me not to run around Taipei they left, saying they would pick me up in the morning. No signing in or people watching you. You were on "scouts' honor." I could have just taken a cab to the tourist hot spots or done anything else I wanted. I didn't, because I was tired and a little apprehensive about getting caught leaving the hotel. In the morning, just as they said, they arrived in their minivan, took me to my airport gate, handed me my passport and wished me a safe journey. Today, there is no visa requirement.

During my many trips to Taipei I could never warm up to it. It is just one of those places I don't feel any real connection to, despite some very nice clients who always tried to make sure I was comfortable.

The famous National Palace Museum (國立故宮博物院) contains the treasures removed by Chaing Kai-shek when he fled the mainland. Many are on display. It is a vast collection that, despite some queries from mainland curators, has never been allowed out of Taiwan, not even one vase or scroll. Apparently, they are afraid that whatever they lend out may not be returned.

Now that the ultranationalist (now jailed) former president, Chen Shui-bian 陳水扁 is out of office, the mainland has begun to lend some of their pieces to the museum, no doubt expecting at some time there will be reciprocity. I would estimate that this will happen soon, just as many of the former restrictions between the two Chinas have been relaxed over recent years. There are now many direct flights from Shanghai and other cities to Taiwan for the many trade and tourist visits. In fact, businesses from Taiwan are the largest single group of investors in China, having financed multiple projects. Such investments are now legal and encouraged. No more need for "noodle shops."

I haven't been back to Taiwan in many years and doubt it will find its way on to my travel agenda soon.

Singapore.

Singapore

It began with vague warnings that there was an unidentified virus which had caused the death of a Singaporean who had recently traveled from Hong Kong. It evolved into an invisible plague that created empty streets, restaurants and hotels. SARS had hit.

"On February 21, 2003 Liu Jianlun, a 64-year-old Chinese doctor who had treated cases in Guangdong, arrived in Hong Kong to attend a wedding. He checked into the Metropole Hotel (the ninth floor, room 911). He felt well enough to travel, shop and sightsee, but the next day he sought urgent care at the Kwong Wah Hospital and was admitted to the intensive care unit. He died on March 4."*

It took weeks for health professionals to realize that this was something different and deadly. It was called the Severe Acute Respiratory Syndrome (SARS) virus. Before it ended in Singapore, there were 238 people affected and 33 deaths. Worldwide there were 8,096 infected in 29 countries, and 774 deaths.**

The relatively small numbers compared to the total population seems minor, but when you don't know what is causing it and people are dropping dead, there is general fear and apprehension.

What should I do? Can I go to public places or should I just stay home? Can I tell if I am in the early stages? Does it float in the air? How do you get it? No one knew. All these questions were on everyone's mind.

---

*Wikipedia, abridged and edited.

**Health Promotion Board Singapore; US National Library of Medicine National Institutes of Health.

Lee Kuan Yew
"founding father"
of Singapore.

As it crept through the country, schools were closed. Theaters cancelled performances. Movies stopped showing. Subways ran without their usual passengers.

During the epidemic, one of the saddest moments for me was going to dinner at a friend's new restaurant and finding it completely vacant except for the owner and his wife all alone in a corner table. They had set up this restaurant at great expense only months before, and now it was empty. It was financially devastating not only for them but for almost all public accommodations. Hotels had 20% occupancy, entertainment venues were shut, restaurants and those stores near schools and the universities were closed, even the ubiquitous food courts and *kopitams* had few regulars.

My friends at Ya Kun, one of the most famous Kaya toast and

coffee joints, gave free breakfast and coffee to cabbies. Fear, courage and generosity were all present. The emergency lasted for three intense months, but gradually we and the rest of the world came out of it.

The Singapore government acted with speed, efficiency and decisiveness, just what you would want from a government at such a time. There are very few nations that could have acted so decisively.

They told us all to take our temperature twice a day, every day, and they sent everyone an electronic thermometer. A rising fever was one of the early signs, but, of course, not definitive. Those who were suspected of developing SARS, who had been exposed to a family member who had come down with it, were quarantined to their homes. If they were found to have strayed, they were fitted with an ankle bracelet that tracked their movements. If they still didn't obey, then they were thrown in jail.

Medical workers who had roommates who worked in a different hospital were told to separate, and only those from the same hospital could room together. Cabbies were required to post their temperature in the cabs twice a day. If they didn't, their GPS was shut down and they couldn't get calls. TV monitor screens were put in the airport that electronically took everyone's temperature and displayed it in a little bubble above their image as they came off planes. If it was not normal, they would be taken aside and examined by a doctor. Actually, it was quite interesting to watch the screen as people passed. You also had to turn in a card as you left your aircraft, telling the exact seat you were in and the address and phone number where you could be contacted in Singapore, in case someone on the flight came down with SARS. Schools had been closed temporarily, but on April 5th, school closure was extended. This was over a month and a half after the first outbreak, and we were still in unchartered waters. The Singapore government's work was smart, thorough and complete, but not over.

I happened to know the head of immunology for the whole country. All during this time, she would have telephone conferences with all the health institutes throughout the world and compare notes for what had transpired that day. Even the tiniest improvement in any reported cases were encouraging. I also knew one of our Spirit of Enterprise awardees, who was a brilliant scientist and before it was all over, she had developed a test for identifying the virus. In some ways, it was as if everyone was operating in the dark, groping for clues as to what could be done both to identify the virus and to protect against it. Masks and gloves for the medical workers were discovered to work very well.

Early on, the government, through a privately established nonprofit initiative using the medical societies, started a fundraising drive, labeled the "Courage Fund," to highlight the courage of the health workers who were essentially "flying blind" in the beginning, not knowing how to protect themselves, how to identify real SARS patients and what exactly to do when they were identified.

They hoped to raise a few million dollars to alleviate the costs to health workers and their families who either contracted SARS or who had a family member who did. Most of the deaths in Singapore were health workers trying to save others. Singaporeans opened their purses and wallets and, with unbelievable generosity, gave over thirty million dollars. It was a tidal wave of concern from people who didn't normally give to charities because the government funded most social programs. I don't know anyone who did not contribute, from my cleaning woman to some of the wealthiest in the land.

When the Courage Fund had been set up, it said it was for the 795 families who were affected by SARS, especially the medical workers.* Over a two-year period they expended about $2 million for these purposes. So then what about the rest of the

---

*www.couragefund.com.sg.

Street vendor in his shop.

contributions? Instead of asking the contributors what should be done with it, including returning donations, the Courage Fund went on to give funding to a variety of projects, all probably worthwhile, but not why we had all donated. For example, they created visiting professorships, bursary awards, healthcare humanity awards and on and on.

A few years after SARS had passed I challenged the Courage Fund to return unused donations after all the criteria for fundraising had been met. The *Médecins Sans Frontières* (MSF), Doctors Without Borders, had done this after the great tsunami in 2004. This proved to be a good illustration of why Singapore's government needs more flexibility. I wrote to the Courage Fund and got no response. I then wrote a Minister whom I knew, and this elicited an invitation from the chairman of the fund to come and have tea. That's about all it was. A symbolic pat on the head: don't bother us; we know best. A syndrome of some of Singapore's leadership and the arrogance of power.

Undeterred, I went to a member of Parliament who was also a doctor and the chairman of Raffles Medical, Dr. Loo Choon Yong. We had become friends when we worked on a government committee to suggest ways to improve Singapore. He was very connected to the leadership. He agreed with me, and asked me to prepare a presentation for his raising it in Parliament. I did, and he did. We prepared an ironclad syllogism of why this entity shouldn't be using the donors' money the way they were. It was very critical, but absolutely accurate. The Minister overseeing the medical societies was upset and asked Dr. Loo if I "was a troublemaker." I wish he had said, "Yes," but he didn't.

That afternoon I called the press since it was a public session of Parliament, and gave them the story, which was reported the next day. A few days later, my friend Doctor Loo called me and said, "Ok, that's enough; they get it." I have no doubt the prime minister sent that message. The end? No, the Courage Fund essentially has done nothing except to be more transparent about what they are

Thaipusam, Hindu holy day , Singapore.

The Flower Dome conservatory at Gardens by the Bay, Singapore.

doing. That's Singapore. It will change though.

In a later conversation with another Minister, Vivian Balakrishnan, I said, "Oh my, if you don't like what I'm doing … poor me, you might deport me to the United States." Just like Br'er Rabbit not wanting to be thrown into the briar patch! We both had a good laugh. Unfortunately for native Singaporeans, challenging the government isn't a pleasant experience, to say the least.

It is curious that senior government officials are, in the main, really talented and dedicated people. The crème de la crème of public service, they have this overarching belief that what they are doing is the way it needs to be done, and are very resistant to outside input. This may be because of several factors, one of which is that they probably have thoroughly researched and vetted the subject, and hence feel that they have looked at all reasonable angles. There is also, especially with the "top of the heap" ministers, a taint of arrogance. Not all of them; certainly minister Balakrishnan wasn't like that. He is an ethnic Indian in a Chinese cabinet.

The most egregious example of arrogance I saw from a minister was a verbal dispute that arose during a friendly luncheon with about ten others. He proclaimed that the USA didn't allow dual citizenship. I told him that indeed it did, but he wouldn't hear of it. Later I went back to my office, pulled up the official U.S. State Department site that clearly stated that the U.S. does allow dual citizenship and sent it to him with a polite note. His response: "no, but … etc., etc.," trying to justify himself. He just wouldn't accept being wrong.

Another example was when I, along with others, was asked to help the now president, Tony Tan, draft a speech encouraging entrepreneurism. I said to tell the students to "challenge authority." He looked at me like that famous W. C. Fields photo of him slyly looking over his poker hand. I'm sure he was thinking, "How did this guy get in the room?"

Dragon Boat Race, Singapore.

I lived in Singapore for seven years and enjoyed almost every day. What is not to like, since they invited me to be on several important government committees, gave me a medal, the *Pingat Bakti Masyarakat* (Public Service Medal) and welcomed me as a Permanent Resident.

Part of belonging to Singapore is to let the warm equatorial weather be a joyful part of your daily life and not resent it as some visitors do. These visitors only venture from one air-conditioned venue to the next.

The nights are especially enchanting. One of the wonderful walks is from the Esplanade walkway along the convergence of the Singapore River and the Kallang River catchment, rebranded as Marina Bay, up to the Cavenagh footbridge, and follow along the Singapore River at least to the Asian Civilisations Museum, one of the "jewel" museums in the world. A stroll a bit further leads past the old Parliament building up to the North Bridge road bridge.

This is a totally free city-state—except you can't mess in politics if you are foreigner. You can't even give a political donation, something I wished to do for one of my friends, a member of parliament and minister.

Singaporeans can form political parties and run candidates for election. There are many hurdles the ruling People's Action Party (PAP) puts in front of you, but at the end of the day, Singapore is a functioning democracy with heavy-handed management from the top. This evolved from the early days in 1959 when it wasn't at all sure how things would turn out and there was a strong Communist Party trying to become the ruling coalition.

Lee Kuan Yew, the George Washington of Singapore, is quoted as saying, "I carry my own hatchet." He used it to crush the opposition, and set up one of the most prosperous countries in the world. Even China, when Deng Xiaoping took over, came calling for advice. Years later a story circulated that when Lee Kuan Yew was in China he had publicly mentioned many improvements that he thought should be made. When this were reported to Deng, he apocryphally said, "I greatly admire Prime Minister Lee, and if he lived here I would give him a small city to run."

In Singapore, some people feel that the government listens in to your phone periodically, especially to foreigners. What a boring job, if it really exists.

My home was quite close to Speaker's Corner, which had been established to let people vent their views, except that foreigners cannot speak and those who want to speak have multiple "can'ts" and "musts." Can't deal with religious subjects or "or any subject which may cause feelings of enmity, hatred, ill-will or hostility between different racial or religious groups," can't speak without registering, can't use high-powered microphones; must sign up one's intention to speak in advance at the attached police station, must speak only in one of the official four languages or related dialects of Singapore.

Actually, none are onerous or even unreasonable. They are not exactly like Speaker's Corner in London. Here the government is absolutely super sensitive regarding religious and racial matters that may cause disharmony. In 1964 there were two race riots between Chinese and Malay Singaporeans. For good reason it energized the leadership, who then and there decided no such thing would ever happen again. It could ruin Singapore, a small city surrounded by two large neighbors, Malaysia and Indonesia. This was the year before Singapore was thrown out of the Federation of Malaysia. There was a fear of the Chinese population causing an overthrow of the Malaysian political elite, who were afraid of the effectiveness of the Singaporean-Chinese-dominated PAP as a political force.

Unfortunately, in less than four years riots broke out in Malaysia against Chinese Malaysians. As my Chinese driver in Kuala Lumpur years later told me, "I carry two passports." I asked why. "Sometimes they kill us."

Today, both countries are very careful about protecting their ethnic dominance.

Singapore is always alert and sensitive to its size and vulnerability. It was really annoyed when the president of Indonesia pejoratively called it "a little red dot on the map." Funny enough, this insult has become a point of pride with Singaporeans.*

I had a very good seven years. One of the things that made it so successful, was that the government, once they spotted you, and figures out you have something to offer, invites you to make a better country by inviting you to serve on various boards and committees aimed at improving some aspect of national life.

What is different, at least in my experience, is that the government listens to the recommendations of these boards. For example, I was on a board whose sole task was to seek out old business and finance laws that no longer served their intended purpose and indeed now obstructed commerce. We identified many and, lo and behold, they reviewed them and then sent our recommendations to Parliament to do away with them.

They also listened to ideas that they had resisted in the past. We suggested an over-the-counter stock market, which in various countries is the traditional first step for a growing company to get capital. This is inherently risky because many of these companies are quite small and often don't do well over the long term. Singapore is risk-averse for its citizens, especially using their spare investment funds. Over-the-counter markets are often referred to as "curb" markets because they often start with buyers and sellers outside on the street gathered together. This is exactly how the New York Stock Exchange is supposed to have evolved. We

---

*"Little red dot" is an epithet that describes the manner in which Singapore is marked on many world maps. It was apparently used to refer to Singapore in a disparaging manner by former Indonesian President B. J. Habibie, and has come to be used with pride and a sense of the nation's success despite its physical limitations. – Wikipedia, with edits.

presented our case, and it was accepted on a very small scale with lots of limits, but, indeed, it was started.

I was on another board whose purpose was to invest in new company projects that had a high probability of failure. Yes, that's correct, a high probability of failure, but were considered worth the try for the innovation they might engender.

As a board member we used to get a fat binder delivered to us a week or so prior to the board meeting, which was prepared by our secretariat. It included the four or so companies that were going to present to us at the board meeting and also all the proposals that were deemed not of sufficient quality to be considered. This second category provided the much needed comic relief from reading through the reports. For example, we had one man who proposed a new government program to eradicate dengue, a fever caused by mosquitoes. After about thirty pages of his obtuse explanation, it turned out to be a fly swatter.

When the first plane hit the World Trade Center, I got a call from Ann Miller in the United States who said, "I think a private plane just crashed into the World Trade Center; turn on your TV." By the time I did, the second plane had hit, and we all knew this was something different. It was night in Singapore. It was 9/12.

Being far away from home made me feel closer to my country, than I normally did. It is events of unusual importance that elicit a feeling of belonging and patriotism. The next day, on the way to my office in Raffles Place, a TV crew spotted me and headed in my direction. I waived them off. They understood. Americans were in mourning. Give us a little time.

The Government of Singapore responded magnificently, not just with the normal diplomatic statements, but they organized a memorial service in the National Stadium a few evenings later.

My expectation was that maybe a few thousand Americans would show up, and maybe some of the government ministers. I wanted to go and share my grief and determination with those few who would participate. When I walked into the stadium I was dumbfounded. It was jammed—and not primarily by Americans or Europeans but Singaporeans. Just folks there to say they were sorry about what had happened to their friend, their ally and ultimate protector. The whole government showed up, including the Prime Minister Goh Chok Tong, Lee Kuan Yew and the entire cabinet.

The ceremony itself was a combination of multiple religious leaders offering prayers with the head of the American Chamber of Commerce offering a touching tribute to all those who perished. There were other short tributes and inspirations, but the most moving part of the ceremony, besides the crowd, was at the end, as candles were lit all over the stadium and everyone sang. I don't remember what the song was but it didn't matter; we were all together.

Every day is sunny in Singapore, albeit with a quick torrential rainstorm in various parts of the island. The Central Business District (CBD) gets less than the more rural areas, but often the rain lasts about five minutes or so and comes down in a torrent. To say it has the power of a fire hose is not an exaggeration. When I first arrived, I asked a friend where you could get an umbrella that could withstand such downpours. He said, "a coffee shop, and by the time you are finished the streets will be dry." He was so right, even to the dryness of the streets. That's what being on the Equator does.

This combination of heat and rain makes Singapore a good place to grow certain fruits and vegetables. In the extreme north of the island, in the Kranji countryside, an area most Singaporeans have not ventured to, are farms.

When you think of Singapore you don't think of farms: you probably think of tall buildings and a modern metropolis. That's how most Singaporeans think about it, too. When I would urge locals to go see the farms, they would look at me incredulously and ask if there were really farms in Singapore. There are, and the glory of the farms is Bollywood Veggies.

This is the brainchild of two wonderful people, Ivy Singh-Lim and her husband, Ho Seng Lim. Ho Seng is low key and always upbeat. They created a farm from abandoned government land, built their home, built a restaurant and happily called it Bollywood Veggies, reflecting Ivy's heritage. They then expanded into a center for the study of the history of agriculture for schoolchildren.

Ivy is what we would call a "one of a kind." She is outspoken in a country where many keep their opinions to themselves; she is very bright, sexy and hysterically funny.

It is an effort to eat in Bollywood Veggies and not be kept in stitches the whole time. Their partially open-air restaurant is one huge room looking out onto the farm as it stretches in the distance. All the food comes fresh from their fields. Ho Seng often acts as host—as well as busboy. Patrons, I expect, have no idea he was one of the most respected and successful executives when he ran the largest supermarket chain in Singapore.

I met Ho Seng on a Nature Society bird-watching walk. Neither of us had gone on one before, and about halfway though I found myself at the drag end of the small group as we walked along, trying to act enthusiastic as the leaders spotted this bird or that. Finally, we drifted quite far behind and started to chat. Before long we both, feeling like little kids escaping from some mandatory school event, fled the scene and went and had a drink of cool tea at his nearby home. What an eventful day for me, because they have remained friends ever since.

Ivy, a compatriot, is what we might call a "shit disturber," one that you cheer from the sidelines hoping that she (and you) won't be mowed down by some force of injustice or stupidity. However, Ivy gets you into the fray no matter how timid you may be. She makes us all, as she calls her kitchen staff, "warriors."

Because of Ivy I am a proud original member of the Kranji Countryside Association, pitchforks held high. Some anonymous

Spirit of Enterprise Awards.

officials of the Singapore government decided it would be a grand idea to build a dump down Neo Tiew Road near Bollywood Veggies and close to one of Singapore's truly fine national parks, the Sungei Buloh Wetland Reserve. To the battlements went Ivy and we followed (from behind). Actually I have no idea how our efforts cajoled some bureaucrats to modify their actions, but in Singapore any official recognition that they are accountable in any way to the citizenry is a big deal.

With the Kranji group Ivy has pulled together the whole farm area, where there are all kinds of farms from goat, chicken and even fish farms to vegetable, fruit and the more exotic hydroponic agriculture, not to mention bugs and other crawling creatures.

They have arranged "on and off" buses to circle the area, and Ivy and Ho Seng have singlehandedly introduced not only school children but all the rest of cement-bound Singaporeans to a mythical area of farms.

It is a wonder to see what Ivy and Ho Seng have created. Just wandering the fields and ponds of their property is an experience in tasting and learning. Many a time while visiting, Ivy or Ho Seng will pick something from a bush or the ground and say, "Try

SNAPSHOTS 51

this." You do, and it is sweet or tart or chewy but always new and fresh, expanding your palate. Head for the restaurant later and there will be more combinations.

More of us should follow the inspiration of Ivy and Ho Seng: we should just "Try this."

My many years living in Singapore convinced me that you can have a pleasant, productive and civilized society with mixed races, religions and economic circumstances. It takes a dedicated, honest and attentive government plus civic acknowledgement that sometimes you have to modify your behavior for the public good. As someone once said to me, "I don't like all the rules, but I sure like the results." I maintain my Singapore Permanent Residence ID with good feelings.

Japan

As we approached the inner circle of the Imperial Palace close to the path that leads to the Emperor's private residence, a guard appeared from behind some shrubbery and my companion dutifully took out our credentials and presented them for inspection. This had been repeated several times before as we drew nearer to the inner circle. The guard was dressed in a normal blue police uniform, except that on his collar was the imperial chrysanthemum emblem. He knew very well who we were; indeed my companion was in effect his boss, "Master of the Imperial Household Agency for Ceremony."

We proceeded on our walk and as we came to the pathway to the residence he said, "We can go no further." The walk through the grounds was quite interesting inasmuch as there is no "palace" in the Palace. It is more a park, with a scattering of pretty bland workaday two- or three-story office buildings and a variety of special-purpose buildings, such as the one that contained treasures from previous Japanese foreign "expeditions," plus museums, an art gallery and the special building for *Gagaku*, ancient court music and dance performances.

From outside the Palace a tourist can see several ancient-looking guard towers and, of course, the moat and perfectly fitted curved rock wall. There is a saying that the large stones are so carefully fitted that "even a mouse" cannot penetrate them.

I've been in the Palace multiple times thanks to my longtime friendship with a senior member of the Imperial Household Agency. I met him about twenty years before, when he was just the head of gardens, and he took me to see the bonsai trees that

Tokyo, Japan.

Modern women,
Tokyo, Japan.

were in an outdoor nursery. The trees are held for bringing out when special visitors come calling. One pine, known as *Sandai-Shogun-No Matsu*, is thought to be at least 500 years old and, according to a Wikipedia reference, was first trained as a bonsai by, at the latest, the year 1610. When you see the Emperor on the TV news greeting a special visitor, you can often see bonsai close by. Over the years my friend gradually gained rank, step-by-step, and reached "the top of the heap" several years ago.

We would often have a meal in the old Palace Hotel, which is directly across from one of the entrances to the Palace. Protocol would restrain me from asking him if I could accompany him at the end of our meal or visit, but from time to time he would say those wonderful words, "Would you like to come in?" Of course, the answer was always yes.

A few times he actually sent me a written invitation to a presentation of ancient court music and dance. What I was not invited to, which we often joked about, was his regular Saturday tennis matches with the Emperor. I asked him if he ever won, and he said, "of course not." "What about when the senior and junior Presidents George Bush played doubles with the Emperor and Prince—who won that?" "The Emperor, of course; it was all pre-arranged." We had to laugh.

From my observation of the Emperor, having met him once and seeing him walking around the Palace and actually sitting next to him at a Palace musical function, I've concluded that it's no fun to be Emperor. One illustration of life in the Palace was my reading about the Empress and her daughter-in-law sort of "going round the bend" in some kind of depression brought on by the structure of Imperial life.

A Japanese friend of mine who is a very close friend of the Emperor—and indeed dated the Empress before the Emperor did—told me that his phone rang one evening a few years ago and it was Empress Michiko. In a conversation with his wife they

Amanohashidate, Japan. Chionji Buddhist Temple.

Arashiyama Sagano Scenic Train station.

Commuters, Tokyo.

reminisced about when they were children and a special pastry shop that baked a roll she loved.

This was a signal to please see if that shop still was around and could her friend pick up some rolls for the Empress? None of this was explicitly said. Often in Japan, things are obliquely referred to without a request being made, but you are expected to get the hint. Anyway, the lady went to the shop and got the rolls and took them to the Empress in the Palace. Couldn't the Empress just go get them? Apparently not.

There is a path in the Palace that goes down a little hill, passes a small lake and then winds upward back into the main walking area. This is the only place that the Emperor and Empress can be completely alone during the day. They take a morning stroll here almost every day. There is another spot which has a very small rice field, and at planting season the Emperor gathers some visitors and plants some rice. Next to the field is a one-room wooden building where Hirohito used to do his marine research, and you can see some old tools that look like they were used in that era still lying around awaiting his return.

Another disadvantage of being Emperor is that you don't have any income or property. In contrast to the British or Thai monarchs, the Japanese monarch is totally dependent on the Diet (Parliament, *Kokkai*) to appropriate funds for the running of the Imperial family.

Having lunch in the large cafeteria where the workers of the Palace gather to eat I was asked during lunch by the head of finance of the Palace how the Thai king got his income. I had extensive experience in Thailand gained when I was trying to buy some Thai insurance companies, and I also had a connection to the royal household. The answer was Crown Properties: the Thai king owns businesses and gets income from them. The finance officer said, "We have no money."

The cafeteria reminded me of what you see when you watch an

Husband and wife tending their crops, Yabe, Japan.

old movie of a Hollywood back lot and its cafeteria. There, set builders, painters, ancient Romans, and costumed "Indians" can be seen all mingling with great stars. A cacophony of clashing images. You can see this same kind of array in the Palace cafeteria: men dressed in formal striped trousers and tails, standing in line with plumbers and little children dressed as "Little Lord Fauntleroys," wearing court presentation outfits. What makes it more amusing is that this is all in the confines of the Imperial Palace, which on the outside is imagined as all ceremony, reverence and deep bows.

One of the buildings that intrigued me was the one that was designated to house all the booty taken over the thousands of years of wars and occupation of foreign lands. I was quite interested in seeing what they had. I asked my friend if we could go in. He said, "Yes, but there is nothing there." "What?" "In 1945 your army brought trucks and took everything." Let me guess, I bet some of those items now reside in the great museums of the world. I know for sure that a famous Chinese Iris scroll that was "liberated" in China by a Japanese general was sold and ended up being exhibited in the Asian Art Museum in San Francisco.

Japan is more than Tokyo, and through a long-standing friendship with the Onishi family, I was able to spend a month in their now vacant home in Kyushu in the village area of Yabe, which I had visited twenty years before.

Mr. and Mrs. Onishi had moved to Kumamoto, which is about two hours away on the coast, and came back only when he conducted services in the temple that was attached to the home. Mr. Onishi is the twenty-second in a line of Buddhist priests, and for many years has been the main priest in this little farming community. His son-in-law has now taken over the duties. This leaves the home quite empty for long periods.

I had mentioned to Akiko, his daughter, that someday I would like to spend about a month in a rural spot in Japan just observing spring. She said, "You must stay at our house; no one is living there now." After many demurs over possible trouble I might cause

Children dressed for a wedding.

Yabe, Japan. Cabbage growing on high mountain.

(what if I burnt it down, what if something happens) I realized she really meant it and, indeed, that April I went to live for a month just to simply observe spring.

Why were there twenty-two generations of this family priests? As explained to me in another context, those who were on "the wrong side" in the battle of Sekigahara changed their lives and withdrew from public life. This battle, fought in 1600, determined the course of history in Japan for the next 268 years. It ushered in the Tokugawa Shogunate, thus minimizing the role of the Emperor.

Even today people know on which side some families were on. It

.Boys Day, Yabe, Japan.

is incredible. Once when I was in Tokyo being shown the way to the office of a former classmate, my guide asked whom I was seeing. I told him, and his immediate response was, "Oh yes, his family was on the wrong side in the battle of Sekigahara."

The area around Yabe is dedicated to farming, and many members of the younger generations have abandoned the countryside for the city, just as Mr. Onishi's daughter Akiko had. Here and there are abandoned homes that I was told could not be sold because "no one wants to live here."

I imagine there are many rural areas in Japan like this. Being located in Kyushu makes it even more remote. It was peaceful and lovely for me to be in this area and observe the unfolding of spring.

I had experienced many springs in Japan since the mid-1980's, and over the many years I had done business in Tokyo I used to come at least twice a year, or even more often, to some area I hadn't seen before, and eventually could boast of having been to the most northern, southern, eastern and western parts of the main islands of Japan.

I even climbed Mt. Fuji. However my observation of spring had generally been to glance out of a car taking me to some business appointment in Tokyo, see the blossoms and ask when we would arrive at the business meeting. I wanted to see what it was really like just to do nothing but observe.

As I have described in my book *Spring*,* my time was transformative. Each day I would slide open the paper walls to enjoy the pruned garden and the gradually changing weeping blossom tree (*Shidarezakura*). This tree, with its long drooping branches, could be compared to a weeping willow, except that this one presented the most beautiful cascading pink blossoms.

---

*Spring: Engaging Nature's Renewal in Rural Japan (Lulu Enterprises, 2007).

Schoolgirls, Yabe, Japan.

The small roads in the area lent themselves to long walks each day. I had no computer, Internet, WiFi or anything like that. I wrote a journal with a pen and paper and took loads of photographs of daily life in the area.

Neighbors who would see me walking along the road would universally greet me and often would mention the Onishi family name, thus identifying where I was staying.

It was not by chance that they knew who I was. The first day I came to stay, Mr. and Mrs. Onishi and Akiko came for a few hours to show me how everything worked in the house and introduced me to the local "mayor" and police station. That information, I am sure, was quickly spread to the neighbors, so they would not be concerned with a *gaijin* (foreigner) wandering their area.

A "neighbor" in my house was "Mr. Mouse," a very small gray and white field mouse who periodically visited the warmest room I was in and sought unsuccessfully, because of my hysterical yelp, to

Couple in park adjoining Palace Hotel, Tokyo, Japan.

My home and temple in Yabe, Japan.

Yabe, Japan. My room.

join me under the *kotatsu*, a blanket-type table under which you put your legs to keep warm.

A red fox would also make his appearance some nights, trotting along the small walkway between the house and temple.

All in all, what this made such a transformative time was letting spring seep into my consciousness, and observing the huge upheaval of soil and water and trees and plants and, indeed, people's lives, as they planted, had babies and began the renewal of life that spring brings. We miss so much in cities.

One of the things I liked doing was trying to emulate Japanese haikus. Not in exact meter, but in the simplicity of the thought or emotions expressed. So I will end this section with one from Yabe.

> Chopping wood sounds
> in the far distance:
> country life.

Indonesia

Suddenly the driver floored the accelerator and we sped James Bond–style down a street, screeched around a corner and abruptly came to a halt. I was being driven to an appointment in Jakarta. "What happened," I asked the driver. "I saw people at the end of the block gathering and it didn't look right." Glancing at the floorboards at my feet, I noticed a small machine gun had slid from under his seat to mine. I realized that I hadn't just gotten a driver: I had a bodyguard. It was time to get out of town. It was May 1998, and Indonesia was falling apart.

It is quite strange being in a country that you know is collapsing, but all the outward daily signs are normal. There is a very odd calm. You hear on the radio that a crowd is gathering at such-and-such a spot, and you just avoid it. You see smoke billowing in the distance from a fire, and you stay away. You go to appointments and meetings doing your normal routine, until it really hits you that your reactions better take a reboot: that it is dangerous despite the outward apparent normality of the day.

One of the nasty things that began as people started to be evacuated were gangs, who were stopping cars on the way to the main airport and holding them up because they knew people would have lots of cash and valuables as they fled. Fortunately for my local staff I had arranged some seats in a medevac plane that was fueled and ready to go from an undisclosed military airport.

The final denouement came when the country opted not to continue the one-man rule, and transformed itself into a democracy. From the USA one late night in 1999, I tuned my computer to a local Jakarta radio station and listed as the new

Denpasar, Bali, Indonesia. Hindu prayers.

Parliament, vote by vote, chose its first democratically elected president, Abdurrahman Wahid, a blind Muslim religious leader of the wonderfully named National Awakening Party. He later got rid of the prejudicial laws against Chinese Indonesians.

It was really emotionally moving after all the turmoil and death to see Indonesia emerge as something completely different from its past, and so it remains more than a decade after that thrilling evening.

Until President Obama, Indonesia was known, if known at all, by Westerners as the land of Bali, that almost mythical idyllic place for honeymoons and liaisons. Maybe they even used the slang "java" for coffee without knowing it referred to the largest Indonesian island.

In our long-ago history classes I'm sure there were a least a few minutes on the "spice islands," where the British and Dutch warred for years over a few islands that they thought grew the only nutmeg in the world. This, along with the trade in cinnamon and cloves, stimulated a grand bargain in 1667. The Dutch felt they had traded up for some of these islands when they gave away Manhattan. This would not be the first Indonesian deal gone bad, and I have a tale to tell.

In early 1996, my investment fund put some money into a private Indonesian insurance company controlled by the Lippo Group, with whom we already had a prior investment. As I recall, the exchange rate to the dollar was about 1,200 Rupiah. The rate at which you enter and leave a currency is critical, as you will quite soon see. Anyway, in early 1997 the insurance company went public. We had an immediate and substantial paper profit. We were geniuses for about two months—and then the roof fell in.

The famous financial meltdown dubbed the "Asian Contagion" hit in summer of 1997, and spread like a virus through Southeast Asia. Economies collapsed along with governments. Multiple long-standing leaders were swept out of office, including the indestructible perennial leader of Indonesia, Suharto. The Rupiah hit a low of 24,000 IDR to the dollar,* and people lined up outside Citibank to make deposits in one of the few banks that didn't collapse. It was chaotic, and even though we still had our holdings in the insurance company, they were literally worthless.

How does it work? If you exchanged a US dollar and got 1,200 Rupiah in exchange for that one dollar and used that to buy into a company, and later reversed the process to take a profit at 24,000 IDR to the dollar, you now have to put up 20 times the original amount of Indonesian currency to equal your original purchase. Not so brilliant anymore.

The odd thing is that the insurance company in Indonesia could keep running and, indeed, it still is. It is just that it would take our investment forever to get a good return. Even today the Rupiah is at about 9,700.

A relatively routine act really brought it home to me. I went to a food court where I regularly had dinner and before the collapse the average meal cost, in US terms, about twenty dollars—and after the collapse the same meal was about two dollars.

As the economy started stalling, the slow-motion collapse of the Indonesian government was unfolding as well. The government of President Suharto had, over his 31-year reign, gradually evolved into a grand kleptocracy, with his family and favored friends in the forefront.

In early 1998, months before he was forced out, he declared that the awarding of bids on the new superhighway toll stations would be open and fair. It was. His daughter was open about the fairness

---

*Low and high when you are discussing exchange rates can be very confusing. Here low means the value of the Rupiah declined in relation to the dollar. So going from 1,200 to 24,000 means you need many more Rupiah to own one dollar, hence the buying power has declined or gotten lower. The reverse is true as well. The meal discussed took many more US dollars to buy before the Rupiah fell; fewer after.

Bali, Indonesia. Getting ready to harvest the rice.

of her winning the award. This seemed to be one of the matches that lit the fuse of revulsion experienced by the general public. Some parts of the country descended into sporadic rebellion and street chaos. Jakarta, the capital, was no exception.

Sometime later I was at a dinner with Nobel economics laureate Milton Friedman, and had him laughing when I told him in Indonesia I had experienced inflation and deflation all at the same time. You learn economics fast investing in the currencies of multiple countries.

Another event brought the finality of the fall of Suharto personally home to me. I was flying across Jakarta in a corporate helicopter and looked down and saw an extensive home with multiple buildings and grounds. I asked a local businessman flying with me if that was Suharto's home. "Yes, and we used to not be able to fly over it," he said with a broad smile.

The brighter side was that shortly after the crisis my investment bank sold Lippo's insurance arm, Lippo Life, to American International Group (AIG) as Lippo teetered on the brink of financial collapse. This sale saved them.

During the riots that preceded the fall of Suharto, crowds had marched on, and set fire to, Lippo's Karawaci shopping center. A few years later, flying by helicopter into their headquarters, I noticed a new set of buildings next to it. I asked the president of the company, Billy Sindoro, what they were. "They are a marine barracks; no one will ever burn down our shopping center again." The Riady family still had political power after all the changes.

I had previously met the founding father of Lippo, Mochtar Riady, who said to me of the impending turmoil. "My family has three strikes against us. We are Chinese, we are Christians and we are rich."

At the end of the crisis they were still all three.

In some Asian cultures the concept of one wife is vague. There is always the principal wife, but then it gets murky. Muslim Indonesians may have up to four wives but, practically speaking, unless one is quite wealthy it wouldn't happen. Another reason was, as a Muslim colleague told me, "My wife wouldn't allow it." Which brings me to a very prevalent alternative to a second or third wife: a mistress or often temporary mistresses.

During a long, long series of dinners with a potential investment target, I would spend most of the time talking to the young president's wife, while her husband and father-in-law drank bottle after bottle of liquor with the president of my Jakarta business. He was a big guy who could drink well into the night with these guys. This left the wife and me to amuse ourselves while they got very happy.

After multiple dinner conversations we finally got to sex. I asked her if she thought her husband had other women, and she surprised me by saying, "Of course he does; all men do." This woman was one of the most stunningly beautiful and gentle ladies I ever met in Indonesia. Why in God's name would her husband chase other women? She said it was simple, "Men are monkeys." I said, "Don't you care?" "No," she said. "However, if he ever gets involved with someone and it interferes with our family life, I will kill him." I believed her.

Two flower salesladys,
Hanoi, Vietnam.

Vietnam

With my arms firmly wrapped around Lan's waist, her motorbike careened ahead into a four-way intersection where hundreds of other motorbikes were heading at the same time but from four different directions. How can this work? No signals, everyone heading in their own direction. Is it possible to get through?

I can attest that it is. It is a combination of "chicken," skill, courtesy, experience and, especially, catching the flow as different directions deftly yield and proceed. Those of a libertarian bent would find joy in it. This was even in the pre-helmet-requirement days. Easy riders every one.

Young men would ogle and flirt with not-unwilling girls at very close range, families would cluster with three or more on a bike. When you are riding right next to someone in traffic, it is hard to be unpleasant, so people seem more courteous, almost as if they are pedestrians having a bit of fun. I found it most charming to see two girls in their pastel *ao dai* traditional outfits and *nón lá* (leaf hats), one holding an umbrella, feigning oblivion to the cute boys passing smiles. Some say the *ao dai* covers everything but hides nothing, similar, I would say, to the Chinese *qi pao*.

The conical head covering you see on young and old, city slickers and most farm people all over Asia is perfect for keeping the sun off. For the young women on their bikes, it provides shade, along with their long gloves and face masks. All for protection against the sun. They don't want to let their skin lose its whiteness.

This is how I got around Hanoi.* One of my staff would pick me up on their motorbike, or I bargained and hired a motorbike "taxi" guy to take me somewhere. It was always slightly thrilling.

Even when you may have fallen over, which happened once in a while, it wasn't a catastrophe, because it would occur normally at rest when the bike might tip over: just maybe a bruised knee or ripped shirt.

What caused problems was the introduction of a few cars. Gradually, over the four years we had a Spirit of Enterprise office there, more and more cars came onto the roads. They pretty much stuck to the center lanes, but it was like schools of fish swimming next to a hungry shark. They could hurt you. They didn't give way, and you could get killed if you were hit by a car. The joy of the streets began to get a little dangerous.

Nevertheless, despite cars and trucks and two-lane roads, riding in the countryside was still enjoyable. One day I was invited by a group of recent university graduates to go out to the countryside and have a picnic. Riding the roads on motorbikes, great care is taken, as you are constantly being overtaken by or overtaking old trucks, whose braking power cannot be relied upon.

The nearby suburbs provide a glimpse of what, unfortunately, will come to Hanoi: duplicative three-story homes and cement shopping strips. The homes are tall and skinny, I am told, because tax is determined by front footage, so if you make your house tall and thin it isn't taxed as much. Why doesn't Notre Dame in Paris have steeples? Same reason: steeples were the tax measure for the whole building so, of course, if you didn't have any, you wouldn't get taxed. At least that's what a professor in college told me. Interesting how taxes influence design: in Vietnam, for sure!

---

*If you were to look at the Vietnamese words Hanoi should be expressed Hà Nội. This holds true for most of the places; but in English we tend to run the words together.

The countryside fairly quickly discloses fewer buildings and more farms and rice fields. Our small group headed for several well-known fields of flowers, acres and acres of them. This was a joyful spot for the girls to pose for photos for themselves and their friends. We then sped on to a small lake, which was part of a

Boat ferries, Hanoi area, Vietnam.

nature park with wooden-roofed platforms beneath which to picnic. Although I didn't know what all the conversation was about, it was still pleasant to be included. Without fail I found most Vietnamese quite friendly to me, especially university students.

The little matter of the American involvement in the "war of liberation" is never raised. When I would bring it up and try to get some kind of insight, they really offered none or something vague like, "Oh, yes, I think my grandfather was in it."

Even at the notorious Hanoi Hilton, the prison that held many Americans, you have to go through room after room before Americans are mentioned. From the Vietnamese point of view, the Americans just came into the very end of a war of liberation from the French that lasted for decades. It was the French who were the culprits.

I spoke multiple times at the Hanoi School of Business at the University of Vietnam, and never once heard anything but admiration for America. My super executive director, Nguyen Phuong Lan, ended up going to Thunderbird University in Arizona, got her MBA and went to work for Coca-Cola, first at headquarters in Atlanta, and then Vietnam.

Let me give you a little idea what some of these talented people go through to get the education they want. Lan, like many others, came from a very humble background, lived with her family, and worked days and into the evenings for a computer company, and then would volunteer in her "free time" to direct our employees and make sure Spirit of Enterprise Vietnam was on the right track.

She saved her money and applied to the top American business schools, only to be turned down for a visa by the U.S. Embassy. The reason given was "you won't come back." No matter what she said or showed of her links to Vietnam, family, job, husband and little new daughter, the answer from young State Department officers was no.

They hadn't seen the likes of Lan. After being turned down multiple times, and against all the rules, she rescheduled herself for another interview, and when she addressed the startled American embassy official she said, "You have turned me down two times and here is why you should let me go," thereupon giving all her reasons. Contrary to what many officials would do, this one called in the two others who had interviewed her

Hanoi, Vietnam, illusionary chaos of the motorbikes.

Hanoi area, Vietnam.

previously and asked why they had turned her down. Not hearing any compelling reason, he issued her a visa then and there. No wonder she was sought after when she graduated. In my opinion, when the embassy finds someone exceptional like Lan, they should urge them to stay in the United States, not keep them out.

Expenses in those days were quite low from an American perspective, and my cozy second-story walk-up office and staff were relatively inexpensive. This placed the burden on me when I stayed for a week or so not to hole up in a fancy hotel where a few nights' cost approached total monthly expense levels. I therefore stayed in local hotels that cost the equivalent of about twenty-five dollars a night.

Before you imagine bedbugs and dirty sheets, think again. Mostly the hotels were in old four-story buildings with very large rooms with sparse bathrooms and electrical connections. The beds tended to be as hard as a marble block, but you got used to it quickly. There were always large, sunny rooms that often had balconies. I often wondered if at one time they had been someone's home.

What was universally quirky from my point of view was breakfast. The very pleasant server would approach you at your table in the open lobby area and ask, "Do you want fruit, eggs or *Phở*?" *Phở* consists of a nice size bowl of broth, rice noodles, a few scallions or other herbs and usually chicken or beef. If you said, "Eggs," off he went straight out the hotel's open front door, only to return a few minutes later with a steaming bowl of *Phở*. The next day he would again present his verbal menu, and no matter what you answered, he got you *Phở*. I concluded he had no idea what he was asking, but it was merely a polite act, and he would hustle for your breakfast that, of course, would be *Phở*, because that is what everyone in Vietnam had for breakfast. Fortunately, I loved it.

I also found that these small hotels were very friendly and the staff was often family. It was much better than staying at the snazzy French hotels that were at the top of the list in the guide books. The people who stayed there missed a lot. Once, a laundry failed to return a t-shirt, and the front desk said that *I* must have been mistaken. Weeks later, when I was back in the United States, I got a message from this little hotel that, indeed, they had found my t-shirt and would mail it to the USA. I said no, just give it to someone who needs a t-shirt.

The same goes for taking an excursion to Ha Long Bay, bordered by the Gulf of Tonkin and not far from Hai Phong. For those of us old enough to remember, Hai Phong was constantly in the news in the early 70's and there was concern about whether or not we would mine its harbor or drop bombs on the Russian supply ships that filled the port.

Festival march, Hanoi, Vietnam.

Museum guide, Ho Chi Minh City, Vietnam.

Ha Long Bay is one of the wonders of the region, with thousands of finely sculptured limestone mountains worn down to skinny karsts, scattered along the coastline. They are very reminiscent of the mountains along the Li River in Guilin, China, and alongside Phuket, Thailand. You have your choice of visiting by local ships or up-market ones. I went local, and we chugged along for two days, stopping from time to time to look at a cave or rock formation. Breakfast was varied and good. Yes, there was *Phở*.

When I would lecture to the University of Vietnam's Hanoi School of Business, the class inevitably would be about thirty, of which more than twenty were always women. I wondered why, and when I asked the dean, he said, "The girls get it, the boys don't." That can be said of a lot of things, but here it was more a pay differential.

Businesses had not yet recognized that an MBA student had something valuable, and there was little difference in the starting salary from a regular graduate and an MBA. The girls realized that it wasn't the starting salary, it was the tools they learned, so they could advance faster once hired.

Vietnam is still driven by its formative Communist ideology and they are savvy enough to recognize it doesn't make for good economics, but they aren't ready to leap into capitalism like China has. At least not yet. Hence, the businesses operate in a "no-man's land" of conflicting laws and aspirations and tend not to value extra education. No doubt because the very entrepreneurs who created many of the businesses didn't have much education. Just a lot of guts and savvy.

The Hanoi School of Business is not funded by the university, i.e., the government, but rather by its most successful entrepreneur, who created a software company that at one time represented half the value of the Vietnam stock exchange. I might remind the academic freedom brigade and the "tisk tisk" head-shakers that this is exactly how Stanford University started.

It was always a joy to speak to these students, and the language used is English, the language of business worldwide, although I remember when I was lecturing Japanese businessmen, I often said the language of the world was Arabic numerals.

The Hanoi students had to be proficient in English or they could not complete their degree. They asked lots of questions, and were funny, quick and attentive.

When I was setting up an office it was not what you might expect when doing the same thing in Singapore or even Shanghai. Nothing is quite straightforward. This is in harmony with the disharmony in the government's split personality of communism

Ho Chi Minh City, Vietnam.

and capitalism. You can't get a license as a nonprofit unless you are a part of a government organization, but that is not easy.

You can incorporate as a regular company, which is what we opted for, and just ran it as a nonprofit. We did the same thing in China. So when you rent an office, your business name doesn't fit what you are doing, which seems ok.

The landlord doesn't seem to have a business incorporated at all for renting in the building, a four-story walk-up, maybe once a home on a beautiful leafy street.

As a matter of fact, there is no certainty that the landlord actually owned the building, because you don't pay rent to anyone but her—and in cash. You don't declare it, and neither does she. She may have just had some kind of lease on our quarters—or maybe not.

This convoluted system also worked for the office phones. I never got it quite clear who actually was leasing the lines to us, maybe they were just hijacked off someone else's line, but every so often some guy without any identifying hat or phone company uniform would come into the office purporting to be the telephone company and collect our monthly charges. Of course, no receipt was offered or needed. The phones continued to work.

Taxes, accounting, business reports? Forget it. Cash in and cash out. As you can imagine, at first this really bothered me, but I got used to how things worked.

What didn't work so well was the ability to keep good staff other than Lan. In creating Spirit of Enterprise Vietnam, we needed people who could work on their own and were self-starters. It caused constant voluntary turnover as the people would often be adrift without specific day-to-day direction.

Some of this can be laid at the doorstep of a country in transition. You can't go from rice farmer to self-starting entrepreneur in a few generations and expect no difficulties. My enthusiasm remains, even though when Lan left for the USA we had to shut down. Hopefully, we will begin again when she returns, although she won't be involved as she once was and, indeed, Coke is sending her to Ho Chi Minh City (formerly Saigon, *Sài Gòn*) the commercial center of the country, whereas Hanoi is the political and national capital.

The joy of Hanoi is that it has not completely transformed itself into a slick, modern city. Thus, street food is everywhere. I've already talked about *Phở*, which incidentally, is found with ease with ubiquitous purveyors with their canonical hats and black woks.

Any kind of food you want is available from little shops that barely fit into building openings. No doors, everything in the open, often partially on the sidewalk and replete with three-legged stools that are only a few inches high.

Noodles done in a variety of ways are for sure in many places, but there are many fish dishes, vegetables and things I didn't recognize but ate anyway. The only concern is you can see they "wash" the dishes by hand in cold water, just sort of swiping them around. The chopsticks get the same treatment, so I always order a glass of hot water, not to drink but to sterilize my chopsticks. I am also armed by my multiple-alphabet hepatitis shots.

The other omnipresent activity seems to be karaoke bars, KTV. Karaoke provides lots of entertainment throughout Asia. In Hanoi some of the spots are so popular that they are impossible to book, unless it is done well in advance.

One of my directors was a constant fan and was known far and wide in all the joints and among the *ao dai*–clad hostesses, who are an essential part of the experience. He would insist on taking me and any visitor he had to these places. It was eye-opening.

Generally, just as you entered there would be a double line of girls waiting to be chosen by you to accompany you to the karaoke room. I was startled at one place to have my host pull out a

**Street vendor,
Ho Chi Minh City,
Vietnam.**

flashlight and scan each lady as he went down the line to choose. They didn't react at all, so this must not have been that unusual.

One of the places we went to you chose your singing room and after you were settled, the door would open and maybe ten girls would present themselves, from which to choose your singing companion. Once chosen, the girl would order some drinks and food.

I never paid, but I assume there was a good markup. I don't think you actually paid for the girls; they came with the room charge, but they expected good tips at the end of the evening. So besides providing a bit of singing and urging you to buy more drinks and food, were the girls there for any other reason? I really don't know.

My host seemed to know his way around. Once, after leaving the room and returning, I found him smooching with his "date." I was told that businessmen come to the KTV and, depending upon the place and the price, the girls might go home with them.

The only girl I ever saw outside was the time we left a club and were chatting outdoors on the street. One of the hostesses, who had been singing with us, now transformed into blue jeans and t-shirt, jumped on her motorbike, gave a fleeting wave and roared away into the night.

My friend was a pretty unique guy. He was a computer genius and ran a software company in Vietnam and Singapore. He had "wives" in Singapore, Thailand and Vietnam. I met his Vietnamese "wife" yet never quite knew what she did for a living. We once went to her home, which was on the street floor and, indeed, we sat on cement and ate dinner that was cooked with an open fire and wok. As we sat in a circle around the wok, the food would be dispensed. Very skinny room and hard floor. Not very intriguing, but an interesting experience.

I don't know if they were actually married or not, but I think he had a baby with someone in Vietnam, which would equal the child he had in Singapore. His "wife" in Bangkok was really lovely,

Hanoi, Vietnam young woman keeping out of the sun but not the glances of the boys in pursuit.

and, I gradually realized, was a hooker. He had met her in some dance bar, of which there are a multitude; girls dance with numbers, you choose, they drink and go home with you. Can you imagine?

Other than the enticement of their looks, what about all the diseases they might carry? Good lord. Anyway, he introduced me to this lady as his wife. Chat, chat, what do you do? She didn't quite say it, and actually I don't even remember what she said, but later he explained to me she danced in one of these places and

Halong Bay, Vietnam. Shoe Salesmen.

came home to him at the end of her work very early in the morning. She also traveled to Europe from time to time, and he seemed quite unconcerned. I found it sad that a really stunning girl was putting away her nest egg and probably supporting her parents this way.

A most surprising observation was that it was the families who sold their daughters to the roving buyers, and the mothers and the village imposed no harsh judgment on the girls when they returned a few years later. They provided a higher living standard for the family, and this was considered good and not a detriment to a future village marriage.

When I was an advisory council member of the Asia Foundation, we went to Thailand and gave support to a group of street actors who performed a very touching play about young upcountry girls sold by their parents and brought to the city for prostitution.

Our little acting group's theme was that the clubs and "massage" places should not take young girls. We are talking about ten- or eleven-year-olds or maybe even younger. Their theme was that it was not only bad for the girls (which the buyers didn't care about), but it was also bad for business (which they did care about).

At the time, the now ousted Prime Minister Tanksin Shinawa was cracking down very harshly, some say illegally, on any club that allowed young kids—and they were *kids*. Interestingly, the street theater was not opposed by the clubs, who understood what they needed to do, but by the *tuk-tuk* drivers and other barnacles that lived off of the people who frequented the clubs.

I don't know what happened to my friend's Thai wife, but I expect nothing very good. He abandoned her and Thailand for Vietnam.

Hopefully, we can get Spirit of Enterprise going again with the help of Coca-Cola, because there is real enthusiasm, especially in the south, for creating new businesses. I expect this time around it will be a little easier.

Laos

The saffron-colored robes of the monks could be seen from afar as they stirred the early morning. A long line of monks walked with steady, determined steps along the road in Luang Prabang, pausing, ever so briefly, to receive rice spooned out by the devotees who were scattered along the route.

This was how the monks got their main meal.

I came to Laos as part of a Bangkok Airlines promotion to see the ancient capitals of the region. The air ticket allowed one to touch down at Sukhothai in Thailand, Siem Rep in Cambodia, Luang Prabang in Laos and Hue in Vietnam. I didn't visit Hue.

Luang Prabang is a very small town that still has the feel of a colonial outpost. My guide there asked me how I liked one of the bridges. "Looks OK to me." "Well, you should like it; it was built by the CIA." His wife was the head of the local Communist Party. Unfortunately, Nixon's extension of the Vietnam War came here, and bombs rained down as the war spilled over into Laos and Cambodia.

This little ancient town is at the confluence of the Nam Khan and Mekong rivers, and I guess that's why it was founded. There is a wonderful Wat and a palace museum but, all in all, it is a quiet backwater in contrast to the modernity that sprouts over some of the more famous places in Asia. The central market has loads of just harvested fruit as well as some local fabrics, a few of which I bought. An expat restaurant, a museum and a wonderfully painted Wat, but that's about it. A sleepy place. Not much doing. Maybe a good reason to spend some time there.

Thailand

The large paper lantern tugged at my hands as the candle inside heated the interior air. The upward force finally overcame my grip and softly, quietly, rose into a perfectly clear Chiang Mai night sky. My eyes followed it up and up until it was caught by the invisible currents, soon joining other floating lanterns quietly drifting away. It is a very moving sight, as if you have lifted your spirit to travel with the lantern.

This was the *Yi Peng* festival night, held to receive Buddhist merit and for many to wish away troubles. The *tham bun*, fire lamps, are released on this full moon evening; so many float into the heavens that the sky resembles a sea of florescent jellyfish.

I am in "up country," as it is called: Lanna, the northern part of Thailand. It is far from the city lights and naked dancers of Bangkok. It seems more gentle, and is populated by farming villages. This region has fewer than a million people, compared to over ten million jammed into Bangkok.

That evening I prowled around the grounds where I was staying until I found a small stream, and watched as its currents carried little clusters of flowers and floating candles, smoothly running with the current. These are barely held out of the water by a banana leaf, folded into a little boat as a tribute to *Phra Mae Khongkha*, the Goddess of Water, whose nature, like many derived from Hindu gods, is very unclear. It reminded me of *Bon*, the Japanese festival with floating candles, to remember and wish farewell to the departed. I found that these floating candles and the skyward lanterns really touched me. I don't know if it was because I thought of it as a part of my spirit ascending, or floating

Bangkok, Thailand.

Bangkok, Thailand. Flower power following 2006 coup.

down the stream, or that I equated it with the souls of family members no longer around, or my own mortality and immortality. Maybe all of that. They are images I keep close.

I was here with members of the Asia Foundation to look at some of the projects that had been funded, among them a group of women who had been taught to create small items for the tourist shops that were then sold in various parts of the country.

The day we visited, the women had gathered in a small circle, each making a particular item they did well. We were told that this small effort had added substantially to their almost nonexistent income.

It struck me as unsustainable, or at any rate a very small improvement in their daily lives. I'd seen this kind of small development of tourist-sale items in China, when a group of students I was advising helped some farmers turn their straw into flip-flops for sale at local tourist shops.

From my many efforts at encouraging entrepreneurism I've often talked about the difference in making a living and making a business. Normally just making a living doesn't often create additional jobs, except for a limited number of family members, while even the smallest business tends to hire new people as it grows.

A good illustration of the effect of a small business is the story of three Singaporeans who were among the first honorees of the Spirit of Enterprise. All three worked in Silicon Valley in California for a software company, and they dreamed of creating their own tech company when they moved back to Singapore. Very often these young men would meet at a local shop, talk and drink smoothies.

One day one of them held up the drink and said, "You know, these are really good; I wonder if it would be a good business in Singapore?" Out went the dream of tech and in came the dream of healthful drinks. They subsequently bought the franchise for Southeast Asia, and today they have more than twenty outlets in Singapore and multiple ancillary businesses.

What I really like about the story is this: in each shop it takes about five people to run it. Three of the people have to be well-trained, and are normally quite young. The other two do the cleanup and other tasks, and are usually elderly. Often they are retirees or have been made redundant by high-tech companies and who otherwise couldn't get a job. So you have two groups, youths and the elderly, one hundred people who are making incomes. If the founding three young men had gone into tech, probably these kinds of people would never have gotten jobs. I love this kind of story.

Many times after a lecture at a university, or just talking to young people about starting their own business, I try to encourage them to look at sectors that are demeaned by the smart-ass MBAs who are flocking to consulting firms or Wall Street.

"Get into businesses that others eschew." "Why not try some businesses that not many people are in because they are not prestigious or 'clean'?"

Sometimes businesses that were started by first-generation family members seem too mean for the university or MBA graduate. They feel funny about the fact their father may be in the laundry business or reconstituted oil or farming. My view is this is just the kind of business that often has little sophisticated competition and often has not upgraded for technology or modern techniques, and could be enhanced by the next generation. I'm afraid some of the students are carried away by the glitter of tech and the lure of fast money.

When I was finishing my book on entrepreneurism in Singapore,* my editor eschewed the fact that the final quote was from a goat farmer and hence, with her National University of Singapore background, was not worthy of quoting. "Who listens to goat farmers?" That's the kind of mindset that I would love the youngsters to compete against.

Much of my time in Thailand was spent in Bangkok, the financial and administrative capital. The king is there, as well as the rest of the royal family. I had met the youngest princess and her lady-in-waiting at a social function in the United States, and they had urged me to visit and, indeed, had a yacht in Phuket that they insisted I use when I told them that's where I was headed in a few weeks.

I thought this was just chitchat until the very hour I checked into Amanpuri in Phuket and my phone rang. It was the manager of the hotel where the yacht was kept, and he was wondering when I was coming to use it. I was really dumbfounded, but not enough

*_Singapore's Homegrown Entrepreneurs Tell You How To Do It_ (Landmark Books, 2003).

that I didn't suggest a date and, a few days later, head to the other side of Phuket to meet him and my glamorous yacht.

Gently bobbing, this extremely large yacht, really a small ship, with a fully liveried crew, was waiting for me to board. It was a bit bizarre.

Just me and a crew of about ten. The captain greeted me as I boarded and asked, "Where do you want to go?" I had no idea, so I just left it to him, and sailed we did.

From time to time, the crewmembers would bring me something to eat or drink, as we cruised the Andaman Sea with its many scattered islands. After a lunch, which could have taken care of a handful of passengers, we moored in a lovely little bay, and the crew said they were going to take me snorkeling. Thereupon they lowered one of the small boats we carried, and we motored closer to the shore. They had fins, a mask and a snorkel all ready for me, and once we were in the water, they had a bag of food for the fish so that they would swim towards us. It was wonderful and beautiful. Every kind of multicolored fish came calling. They had no fear, and lounged around as long as we stayed.

Grand Palace, Bangkok, Thailand.

Bangkok, Thailand. Adjusting the wires.

After returning to the ship and yet another small snack, we headed for home. The hotel manager again met me as I disembarked, and said the princess said I could use the yacht any time I wanted. It's nice to know a princess.

While I was in Phuket I learned how easy it is to drown. I had walked down from my hotel to a beautiful beach and taken a swim in the shallows of the Andaman Sea.

Knowing how treacherous the ocean can be from many childhood adventures in Bolinas, a bit north of San Francisco, with its Pacific Ocean breakers and riptides and where a classmate had drowned, I kept my eye on a couple swimming not far from and parallel to me. This way I wouldn't inadvertently go too far out without realizing it.

Within a few minutes they disappeared. "What?" "Where did they go?" I couldn't find them, and then realized I had been carried away from shore by an invisible force. Turning back to shore I headed in with strong strokes. I moved farther away, not closer, and quickly realized I wasn't making any headway at all. "Ok, now what?"

Trying to stay as calm as possible, in a few seconds I concluded that the only way in was to wait for a wave, swim as hard as possible with its force, wait, swim with the next, and repeat this with the hope it would take me to shore. It did.

As I wearily struggled onto the beach, a man in swimming trunks said, "I was just ready to come and get you." Thank goodness; he was a lifeguard and had been watching me the whole time.

Most of the time in Bangkok was spent trying to buy insurance companies, leaving little time for exploring temples, shrines and museums. However, from time to time, but not often enough, I would schedule some weekend days just for sightseeing. One of the side trips I took was to the ancient capital, Ayutthaya,* a few hours up river from Bangkok. It gives a good feel of what Bangkok might have been like in its earliest days.

It is not at all unusual for people to say how "lucky" you are to travel to this or that wonderful city, but the truth is that most businessmen schedule their meetings and fly in and out of these exotic places without observing the unique local attractions.

I have a friend who flies to Paris from Shanghai almost every two weeks for meetings and rarely has had time to visit even the most

---

*Ayutthaya was founded in 1350, and was the second capital of Thailand (after Sukhothai) for 417 years, during which time it was a very prosperous kingdom. In 1767, the city was attacked and burned down by the Burmese army, forcing the inhabitants to abandon the city. Ayutthaya was never rebuilt, and the area has been declared a UNESCO World Heritage Site since 1981. – Wikipedia

well-known sites. It was that way for me, too. Often, I would come to Bangkok with a team of two or three, and we would have multiple visits all lined up with very little time in between. Our schedules even took into account the cement-like Bangkok traffic and set meetings strategically at certain places and at certain times when we knew the traffic would be less congested. If you didn't, you could end up stuck in a car, unable to move even one car length for long periods, sometimes up to an hour, just sitting idling, with no movement. This was before the overhead light rail and the subway were completed.

We were so focused we would just want to do our business and get out. Finally, I insisted that at least a half-day be scheduled for exploring.

We got to know many insurance companies and investment bankers in Bangkok, but in the end never were able to make the kind of investment we thought would be fruitful. We did get to know some really fine people and gain an understanding of some of the customs and traditions of Thailand.

There were some especially greedy generals in the way of our efforts to make some inroads into purchasing parts of Thai companies. These were self-directed owners with false real-estate values and, by the way, were not the only hindrance we faced.

We had to be alert as well to factors that might impact a life insurance company, such as HIV/AIDS, since Bangkok, the main population center, had its notorious sex worker population. When we looked at the data in one of the larger companies we found a surprising result. HIV/AIDS was much more prevalent in the Golden Triangle, north at the border with Myanmar, than in Bangkok. The reason was the drug addict population in that area and its sharing of contaminated needles.

There were several other detriments to becoming a shareholder other than the overvaluing of assets. Less easily revealed was the reluctance to have non-Thais own a significant share of a local

Bangkok, Thailand. Preparing an awareness event at a shopping center.

company. No one ever said it directly and, actually, there were legitimate ways you could even buy control of a Thai company, but there it was, unspoken.

Overvaluing of assets remained a problem for some time. Ever since the financial "Contagion" triggered by the spiraling collapse of the Thai Baht in 1997, real estate values had dropped to twenty percent, or even lower, than their former valuations. Many Thai companies refused to acknowledge this and kept these assets at their original acquisition prices. This directly affected the ability to write new business and, especially, to pay current claims.

When I pointed this out to one CEO and observed that he couldn't pay claims with "bricks" he merely looked at me. What I later realized was he didn't plan to pay claims anyway! All this

Bangkok, Thailand. Military officers.

stuff is very tricky from many different angles and obviously a sensitive issue to the management who got the companies into the pickle in the first place. One story I heard was that of an owner of an insurance company who was also an officer in the Thai army. He sent all the damaged cars that he had insured to the local army repair garage. Money passed all around.

One of the few companies that faced up to every challenge happened to be run by a woman. This was very unusual at the time, and she was the only woman running a major company, at the time called Samaggi Insurance PCL.

Today there is a female prime minister, Yingluck Shinawatra,* and

---

*Sister of former prime minister Thaksin Shinawatra, who was ousted by an army coup in 2006.

there has even been talk of a queen. Women had not been seen in Thailand or, for that matter, in many parts of the world as having a role in "men's affairs," as a local man put it to me.

On my very first visit to Thailand in the mid-1980's, I stayed at the Mandarin Hotel, which is not only the pride of the Thais, but also of Jardine Matheson, the ultimate owner.

Today's hotel has a multistory glass main building, but the cognoscenti always want to stay in the old building. This is where many authors wrote their most famous books, including Somerset Maugham's *On a Chinese Screen*. I had a two-story suite that faced the busy Chao Phraya river and its loud, exposed-engine "long-tail" boats and, across the river, the lovely *Wat* (temples) with their unique designs.

This hotel has three connections for me: Somerset Maugham's book; Jim Thompson, the founder of the modern Thai silk industry; and the wonderfully generous wedding reception of my friends Jan Pijiayachan and Poh Suparoek.

In a glass case, the hotel gratefully exhibits books written by Maugham and those of other authors, like Joseph Conrad and Graham Greene. Somerset traveled through Asia in the 1920's and made a series of notes for a book he intended to write about China. He never wrote the book, but collected the notes into a series of essays on what he had observed. Inspired by these, I was tempted to follow his lead with this book, but decided not to use that format. The stories he tells give you a brief glimpse of people and activities at the time. If this book is successful, I don't expect it will make their exhibit, but maybe some reminiscent images will linger.

The old Mandarin is painted a heavy cream color and has some of the sensual feel that the whole country seems to produce. I don't know if it is the *wai*, the gentle greeting *"sawat-dee"* with hands held as if in prayer; the many flowers and fruits placed at the omnipresent small Wat-like houses where household spirits live;

Bangkok, Thailand.
Heavy rain approaches.

or is it the aromas coming from various street shrines scattered around like the four-faced Buddha in the Erawan area, with its drifting incense? This floating sensuality may begin from the sultry heat—or the undercurrent of illicit sex. Whatever it is, Thailand isn't Kansas.

Jim Thompson, the eponymous founder of stores he established in Bangkok and which now are found in different parts of Asia, spent lots of time at the Mandarin, sitting on the veranda chatting, plotting and creating an industry with locals. His home, two combined upcountry houses, is now a museum.

A local friend, Jane Puranananda, captures some of the unique fabrics in *Through the Thread of Time* and edited another wonderful book, *The Secrets of Southeastern Textiles.** I just love the variety of patterns of the various items that the Jim Thompson stores now

---

Through the Thread of Time: Southeast Asian Textiles (River Books, 2006); *The Secrets of Southeast Asian Textiles: Myth, Status and the Supernatural* (River Books, 2007).

sell. A former colleague of mine recently invested a substantial sum to expand Jim Thompsons in China. My guess is that it will be very successful because of its high quality and good designs.

The Mandarin is the hotel of choice for many wedding receptions and my friends Jan and Poh had their wedding reception there, which I attended, as did her university classmate Xiaoxiao Zhang. Both Jan and Xiaoxiao had volunteered for Spirit of Enterprise during their master's degree studies at the University of San Francisco. Jan and her family showed us extended hospitality beyond what would be expected at such otherwise busy days. The evening prior to the reception, her parents held a small dinner, which was one of the most delicious I've ever had in Thailand. What I couldn't understand was how they had the time the actual night before the wedding and reception.

It turns out that Thai tradition organizes the actual wedding ceremony weeks, if not months, ahead of the reception. Indeed, there was a making of promises and commitments at the reception, but the actual ceremony had been well before.

One of the most moving parts of the evening reception was when the bride and groom knelt on the floor at the feet of their parents to ask for, and receive, their blessing. Tears welled up, it was so touching.

At the reception there was a screen on which a video was shown of the actual wedding ceremony, to which a very small number of relatives had been invited and commitments were made in the presence a presiding dignitary. At one point a small silk cord was affixed to the side of both the bride's and grooms' heads symbolizing, no doubt, their unity.

A quite different activity then takes place at the new couple's home. The bride's parents lie on the couple's new bed and express how lovely their own marriage has been. After that, the new couple also occupies the bed and expresses their hopes for a lasting bond.

I guess this is much better than the old Chinese tradition of multiple relatives and friends gathering around the wedding-night bed with its curtains closed and expressing exuberant exhortations that lovemaking would commence and be joyful. Fortunately, they then leave, but return the next morning to check the sheets to make sure there is blood marking the bride's initiation, signaling a successful night.

In addition to those at the Mandarin, there have been other memorable moments in Bangkok.

I was asked by a university professor if I would like to attend an exhibit of various nonprofits. She had done some work for me when I tried to set up Spirit of Enterprise in Thailand. At the exhibition center there were many displays, and she directed me to the one for the blind. There was a large tent structure that you were urged to enter and explore, finally coming out the other side.

In I went and immediately was enveloped in darkness. I could see absolutely nothing, not even my own hand. A guide introduced himself and very slowly led me through the exhibit, all of which was in pitch dark. He took me into various rooms and asked what I heard or felt with my arm outstretched, trying to figure things out while not bumping into anything. I gradually could tell there was water flowing, some benches and flowers. After I described what I thought was there, he would tell me what I was "seeing," but, of course, not seeing. This was repeated through three or four rooms, and by the end I did pick up a few signals with my hand or ears and he would then encourage me to try harder and, ultimately, reveal what was there. Finally, I exited the exhibit back into the bright daylight and thanked the guide. Only then did I realize he was blind.

One of the advantages of living in China is being able to vacation conveniently in other Asian countries. I can't finish up without talking about massage in Bangkok. There are some very large, clean, reputable, established businesses that give massages. I've been to a few, and can attest that they are legitimate and well run.

("The lady doth protest too much, methinks.") Why I stress this is that there are many, many more that are not really offering just massage. They offer services well beyond that, and as far as I could tell, other than a few obvious ones, you can't tell if they are legitimate or not. Apparently if they advertise as a "barber shop" that means it is not.

I had an adventure close to where I always stayed on Soi Langsuan, just off Rama I and Ploenchit Road at Cape House, which is owned by friends and was very convenient to the elevated and Lumpini Park.

There was a very well-established massage place, advertised as being about two blocks away down a lovely street, alongside a canal where a free-standing, old-fashioned Bangkok home stood. Was it legitimate? With some trepidation I went in and found it well-lit and full of spice aromas. The lady at the desk was quite pleasant, and I asked for the price chart, which she gave me, and hemmed and hawed around the real question of what was on offer. Finally, she got the drift and said, "No sex." It turned out to be a really delightful setting, and the massages were professional and soothing. It was a safe place to return to—and indeed I did so from time to time.

Yangon, Myanmar. the reclining buddha at the
Chauk Htat Gyi Pagoda getting a wash.

Myanmar

As I raised my hand to point to the office of the National League for Democracy led by Aung San Suu Kui, my guide hastily pushed it down and said, "Please don't point at it. Don't even look." This was the atmosphere in Yangon years ago, before everything changed. Other than this episode and the barriers preventing you from passing Suu Kui's home, there was little to indicate that the army had this country almost totally cowed with its strict regulation of political society. Almost, but not quite.

One of the slightly subversive things to do was to visit the home of the patriot Aung San, father of "The Lady." On the walls of the home are family photos that, of course, include Suu Kui. The generals can't erase the fact of her father being held in great esteem, and his assassination just after British rule ceased is considered a dreadful turning point in Myanmar's path.

It is a story of sadness. At the end of WWII, Myanmar, because of its British heritage and English-speaking elite classes, was tapped to be one of the "winner" economies, along with Ceylon (Sri Lanka) and the Philippines. How wrong everyone was.

This is well illustrated by a guide I had in Bagan, the magnificent plain with thousands of Buddhist temples.* He was a university

---

*Bagan is an ancient city located in the Mandalay Region of Burma (Myanmar). From the 9th to the 13th centuries, the city was the capital of the Kingdom of Pagan, the first kingdom to unify the regions that would later constitute modern Myanmar. During the kingdom's height, between the 11th and 13th centuries, over 10,000 Buddhist temples, pagodas and monasteries were constructed in the Bagan plains alone, of which the remains of over 2,200 temples and pagodas still survive to the present day. – Wikipedia

Bagan, Myanmar.
Temples and Pagodas.

graduate of one of the top schools in Myanmar, and had a physics degree. Why was he acting as a guide? "No jobs." This was not hard to understand. The surrounding village had mostly dirt roads and lots of small shacks along the Irrawaddy River. Many had no electricity or running water, including my guide's. What about his classmates? Same thing.

One day we sat quietly on the top of one of the temples and just listened to the surrounding area. A peanut farmer was in the distance plowing his field with the help of a buffalo, a goat herder with tinkling bells followed his little group as they walked along a dusty trail. That's all you could see or hear. Poor and rural, and you could see for miles.

A slight glimpse of what was causing some of the problems could be seen in the airlines you took both to get to Myanmar and to fly around the country. I was told they were owned by a couple of army generals. The military dominated the economy, and that meant that the few got the spoils. If you are military you could make money. A physics graduate; forget it.

No wonder there was a permanent insurrection in the Shan State area, which borders several countries, including China. Although it was apparently driven by ethnic differences, economics had to play a part. To try to placate the Shan, the military gave them jurisdiction over some of the tourists' lodging places on Lake Inle, a magnificent area with homes, gardens and tomato patches all floating on the lake. A lot of cultivation is done with floating plants: they were doing hydroponics long before it came into fashion a few years ago.*

Another impediment to growth is the drug trade, allegedly run by some of the military.** This is in the infamous Golden Triangle. If you can make a lot of money in the drug trade, why develop the country's infrastructure? Why try to build an economy, so my guide can get a proper job? Pretty sad.

What is not sad are the people themselves. Despite all the deprivation, everyone I had contact with was friendly and positive but, of course, these were people who had at least some kind of job.

One thing that did surprise me was that even among the educated there was a strong belief in the spirit world and its effect on day-

---

*In 1929, William Frederick Gericke of the University of California at Berkeley began publicly promoting that solution culture be used for agricultural crop production. He first termed it *aquaculture* but later found that aquaculture was already applied to culture of aquatic organisms. Gericke created a sensation by growing tomato vines twenty-five feet high in his backyard in mineral nutrient solutions rather than soil. By analogy with the ancient Greek term for agriculture, *geoponics*, the science of cultivating the earth, Gericke coined the term *hydroponics* in 1937 (although he asserts that the term was suggested by W. A. Setchell, of the University of California) for the culture of plants in water (from the Greek *hydro-*, "water", and *ponos*, "labor"). – Wikipedia

**The main player in the country's drug market is the United Wa State Army (UWSA) ethnic fighters, who control areas along the country's eastern border with Thailand, part of the infamous Golden Triangle. The UWSA, an ally of Myanmar's ruling military junta, was once the militant arm of the Beijing-backed Burmese Communist Party. – Wikipedia

to-day activities and future events. This seems to be interlaced with Buddhism, which is represented by startlingly beautiful temples and pagodas found everywhere. The Shwedagon and Botahtaung Pagodas in Yangon are most often pictured in tourist booklets, along with the reclining Buddha at the Chauk Htat Gyi pagoda.

I happened to visit Chauk Htat Gyi the day they were cleaning it, using a swing on a long rope that suspended a lone worker polishing the Buddha's face. This is no ordinary statue. To begin with, the top of Buddha's head is five stories high—and is reclining! The rest of his body is stretched out 195 feet.

A few years ago we all saw on television general rioting in Myanmar led by orange-clothed monks. However, here one can see monks in all shades of garments: red, orange, pink and various hues in between. Pink was the color of the outfits of about twenty women "monks" apparently on their way to bathe, as each had a towel set in the crook of her arm. Their heads were fully shaven and their demeanor joyful, especially when I raised my camera in an "asking" motion to see if I could take their photo.

My other exposure to a group of monks was at a monastery where a few hundred lived and worked. They had one meal a day, and it appeared to be mostly rice. They queued up in long lines as their bowls were filled one by one. "That's it," I was told. No other food for the day.

I guess the only other remarkable thing is that the ladies smear their cheeks with *thanaka*, a white paste from ground bark. It is applied in a big circle on the cheeks, both for beauty and to protect them from the sun.

It was too brief a time to spend in such a splendid country, the one which my Uncle Russ, for whom I am named, fought against the Japanese in WWII. This was part of America's help to China, and was aimed at keeping the Burma Road open so that supplies could flow from British India into China.

Yangoo, Myanmar. Prayers at Shwedagon Pagoda.

I still have Uncle Russ's army shoulder patch with Chinese and US emblems on it. It always surprises my Chinese friends when I tell them about the Americans who fought for China in the war. Troops went back and forth between China and Myanmar.

The famous Flying Tigers' main duty in the beginning of the war was flying the "hump" between India and China, bringing in supplies when the Japanese controlled the roads. The Burma Road didn't get re-opened until very late 1944.

South Korea

The most remarkable act of service I have ever experienced happened in a department store in Seoul. I had been looking for a certain kind of tea that was from Cheju Island in the far south of Korea. The tea is of a jellylike consistency and is made from citron. I had found it originally in a Korean neighborhood store in San Francisco.

After looking over all the teas I questioned a shop girl, who didn't know if they had it; she turned me over to someone else. The new young woman said she knew what I was after, and thought it was a wonderful tea, but they didn't carry it. She followed up with "I know where you can get it; just follow me," and off we went down the escalators to the front entrance, out the doors and down the block to the subway stairs, down the stairs into the subway passage, along some long corridors, up some more stairs and into the basement of another department store, up the escalator to a full display of Cheju tea. There, she handed me over to a sales clerk after saying something in Korean, which from the service I then got must have been "take good care of this gentleman." She smiled, and without another word, disappeared. Wow!

My earliest days in South Korea, well before my Asian investment fund took me there often, were in 1988 to see my friend Jay Tunney, who was starting a retail ice cream business from scratch. What guts.

If I've learned anything about real entrepreneurs, I've learned that an essential ingredient is to never give up. Jay had this and more. Before he was finished about six years later, he had built from his one, yet-to-be-opened ice cream parlor, a chain of over sixty ice cream and hamburger outlets. I remember fondly that we stood like two proud parents in front of the original shop and had a photo taken. He was the parent, not me.

These kinds of photos emerge often when a proprietor like Sam Walton becomes a billionaire and his company is anxious to show just plain Sam in front of his first store. I'm proud of the photo because it shows my friend at the very beginning of a remarkable business adventure. I'm just glad I was there to see it start.

Not many foreigners have done well in Korea. I once asked Hank Greenberg, the remarkable CEO of AIG, "Where aren't you where you want to be?" "Korea and Indonesia," he said. "I'll take Indonesia; Korea is just too hard," I replied. He agreed with me.

Incidentally, I did take Indonesia, and later sold him the largest life insurance company there, Lippo Life. With some trepidation, about a year after the transaction, I asked him how it was going, and he assured me it was going wonderfully.

When I started an investment fund that bought various stocks throughout Asia, Korea was one of the places that had large enough companies in which to invest. We had a very good broker, Miss Kim, who regularly did analysis and follow-up on the companies we owned, but even better, would entertain us at one unique restaurant after another.

Anyone who has ever eaten in a Korean restaurant knows that a variety of dishes are always offered. At the places she took us, I think they would display twenty or more small offerings, followed by beef to be cooked at the table and other dishes from an unending cornucopia in an exquisitely presented variety.

From high on the hill at Hotel Lotte we would descend into the financial area of Seoul. In trying to buy into a Korean life insurance company, our Ascendant Capital, partnering with Zurich Capital, encountered something that illustrates the insularity of Korean business.

The government had put out an offering circular to bail out the fourth largest insurance company, which had severely overextended itself. Nevertheless, it had built one of the most glimmering and tall office towers in the business district. We were there to do due diligence and make an offer, if we thought it worthwhile. It was somewhat a challenge.

We would meet in a very large room, where on one side was our team of six and on the other were about twelve of the top officers and directors of the company and their investment bankers. In very short order, we discovered that the office tower on their balance sheet was overvalued by four times and many of their insurance products were losing money. I remember vividly our asking the CEO why he was selling such-and-such a product, pointing out that for every policy he sold he was losing money. The more he sold the more he lost money. His ridiculous answer was "because Samsung sells it and our agents would be mad if we didn't." No wonder they were bankrupt. Something we had analyzed in a few days that was draining cash out seemed very logical for them to maintain.

While our conversations were going on they would take a break

Looking into South Korea from North Korea at DMZ.

from time to time to discuss matters among themselves as they sat there. They assumed we didn't understand Korean. They were wrong, but we never revealed that one of our team, a Han Chinese as he constantly boasted, was fluent in Korean. It was as if we had a bug planted in their offices. We understood everything.

When it was time to put in a bid, of the four or five possible investor groups looking at the company, our team was the only one that did. Our offer was a sieve of caveats and escape clauses. In the end the whole exercise came to naught, and the head of the Zurich team, not long after, went on to become the finance head of the Hong Kong Mass Transit Railway (MTR).

What was really going on? We realized that the Korean government's tender for bids was a sham that merely wanted to show it put the company to international tenders so it could later hand it over to a favored public utility without any further bids. An inside job all the way.

Other non-Korean businessmen have told me stories of their difficulties in either trying to buy or owning a Korean company. A friend owned a bank and had untoward difficulties of disposing of it without lots of intervention by Korean authorities trying to set things up for their favorites.

If you are going to be successful in Korean business, I guess you have to be armed in battle outfits that are right out of the black *Star Wars* type that the riot police wear. A client of mine had a labor dispute with some of his clerical workers in Seoul, which developed into a lock-out and a confrontation with the aggressive workers. The wooden office double doors were locked. Police were called, but before they could arrive the workers had smashed down the doors and cascaded into the offices, causing damage and injury.

It is not easy doing business in Korea.

Once I asked a friend why the Koreans seemed so confrontational. He said that in his business he had at least one nose-to-nose confrontation a day. "How would you act if on the off years the

Door into South Korea inside DMZ.

Chinese didn't invade and run up and down your country, the Japanese did? You would be confrontational too."

Others have said in jest it is the kimchi. It is hot and fiery like some of the people. One of my team told me that he met a girl in one of the offices and took her out, which led to a night where he said he never, ever had such a bombastic, unrelenting, continuous night of passion from a woman. I wouldn't know.

"Waitress, Yogi-yo! 여기 요!"

"A little more kimchi, please. 이거맛있어요"

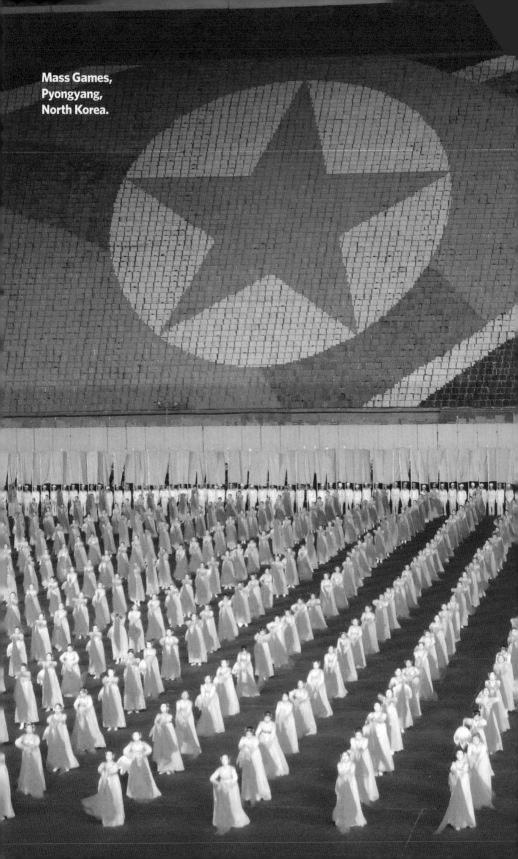

Mass Games,
Pyongyang,
North Korea.

North Korea

I was staring across the 38th parallel. The soldiers staring back were South Korean. It is a very strange feeling being on "the wrong side" of this tension-filled spot.

We had come, compliments of the Democratic People's Republic of Korea, or as the people in the know call it, the DPRK. We picked up on it so we would be seen to be "in the know" when telling of our adventures when we got home.

The "we" was a group of fifteen Americans who had decided for various reasons to enter into the forbidden land. Of course it isn't forbidden at all.

I had seen an ad for travel to North Korea in a Chinese newspaper. It was a tourist agency run by some Brits, and they had been doing the tours for about ten years.

Still not being convinced that it was really possible, I called our embassy in Beijing and was told by an official that they had no objections to me traveling to North Korea. This was especially enlightening since former president Bill Clinton had weeks earlier brought home three Americans who had been jailed for trespassing.

After a few more queries I contacted the tour agency and said, "Sign me up."

To get to Pyongyang you leave from Beijing on a very old Russian airliner run by North Korea's Air Koryo. The passenger cabin was not reassuring. The seats were skinny, the overhead bins so thin a sweater barely fit and fellow passengers, you suspected, were either spies, undercover agents or damn fools like you.

Pyongyang, North Korea music school.
A little individuality in a conformist society.

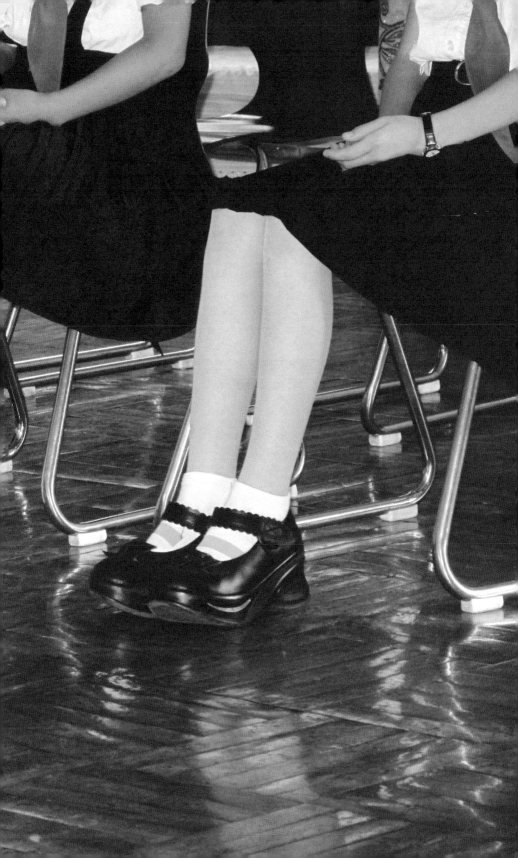

Pyonyang Traffic director.

When we arrived we had five assigned guides—"watchers"—of our little group, one of whom filmed our every move. The really enjoyably one was an attractive young woman in her early twenties.

She had a master's degree in something like tourism and clearly was very smart. I guess it wasn't surprising that someone who was assigned to take Americans around for four days was committed in thought and deed to the regime. Although she began the first day pretty much "by the book," within a few hours her friendly personality shone through. There was an especially fun young man her age who seemed to amuse her; we would have called it flirting in any other context. It was fun to see him try to work his magic on her.

Her English was perfect and unaccented. I asked how she could get a master's degree without the Internet or being allowed to study foreign literature.

"We have the Intranet, just for North Korea." "But there must be some texts you need to study outside of Korea?" "In those few instances I could go to a central place and apply for a certain library to be accessed and a certain text, and the authorities would let me go on the Internet and look at it."

We discussed various things, including her firmly held belief that it was the South that had started the Korean War by invading the North, not vice versa, and how their Great Leader Kim Il-sung had beaten the Japanese into surrender in WWII.

"Have you ever heard of the atomic bomb? "Yes, but Kim would have made them surrender anyway." You get the drift. She has a body of knowledge gathered in a closed society so has no outside references to check if information was correct or not. Just for the record, Kim was thought to be in Russia when WWII ended. At that time Japan had ruled over Korea for the previous forty years.

"Of course I expect the United States to attack us." When I asked why in heaven's name would we would want to do that, she said,

"You want to invade China." If she were not so smart—and so attractive and so friendly—I could have thought she was ignorant. She wasn't. She was just badly informed. I realized after spending some quite enjoyable time chatting with her while our bus headed down the empty four-lane highway to Panmunjom, that trying to persuade her of other views was fruitless. This guide was never exposed to broad outside knowledge in either her field or of the world around her.

I once discussed understanding North Koreans with former governor Bill Richardson of New Mexico, who had taken several successful trips to North Korea. He said the problem with dealing both with Kim Il-sung and his son Kim Jong-il was they had no experience or understanding of the outside world. He added, "Plus they are nuts."

I had brought a small music iPod with me, as it was one of the approved items, along with "single shot" cameras. Phones and video cameras had to be left at home. I expect they knew almost all cameras were not single-shot and could take video as well, but that wasn't acknowledged.

I asked her if she would like to borrow the iPod to listen to some symphonies, which she had said she liked. I pointed out that also on the iPod was Obama's book, *Dreams from My Father*. I asked if she wanted to listen to that as well. She said no. When she returned it three days later I took a look at what she had played and indeed she listened only to the music. No Obama.

I asked her if she was ever able to travel outside the country, and she said that when she achieved a higher rank she could. "Where?" "Beijing." I had to laugh and said, "How about Paris?" She smiled the smile of a knowing girl.

Before we entered North Korea our group was given an hour lecture on "do"s and "don't"s, including what we could bring in and what we couldn't. We were told we couldn't take photos of any military person or out of the bus windows. Don't fold the

Pyongyang. Soldiers preparing to enter the Kim Il-sung Mausoleum.

newspaper in your hotel room because inevitably every day there will be a photo of Kim Jong-il, and it would be considered an insult to the Dear Leader, from which harsh consequences might ensue—such as we might all be kicked out of the hotel.

We had to bow at the large imposing statue of Kim Il-sung and place flowers at the base of it. We had to do the same at his "preserved" cadaver on display in their specially designed sarcophagus, looking just as waxen as Mao or Ho Chi Minh (both of whom I had seen). After a few days into the trip it appeared almost all the "don't"s were overlooked by our handlers, including taking photos of soldiers who at times happily posed with us.

The trip consisted of staying three nights at the Yanggakdo hotel,

Mass Games, Pyongyang, North Korea.

which is on a small island in Pyongyang's Taedong River. It is a decent "no frills" hotel for foreigners. We were told we could not stray from the grounds, although with only one bridge and the river on all sides, I'm not sure where we could have gone anyway.

The countryside was especially delightful because there were no monuments to bow to, no propaganda exhibits or memorial parks: just lovely scenery and some ancient ceramics.

Not far outside Kaesong is the tomb of the 14th-century Koryo-dynasty king and his Mongolian wife known as the Hyonjongrung Royal Tomb, two burial mounds situated high in the hills overlooking a beautiful valley. It is under consideration as a world heritage site.

Not far from there we were able to take a nice hike into the countryside and ended this part of the trip at an old Buddhist monastery, where we were served tea.

In Pyongyang, the propaganda was continuous with the Arch of Triumph, the enormous bronze statue of Kim Il-sung, the Children's Palace, followed by the *USS Pueblo*, the Korean War Museum, Kim's humble country home, his catafalque, and the very spectacular Mass Games.

The Mass Games are really unbelievable, presented in the May Day Stadium, said to be the largest stadium in the world. That I believe. There are more than 100,000 participants in a combination of music, light show, gymnastics, acrobatics, dancing and the greatest card stunts anyone has ever seen, including those on display at the Los Angeles Coliseum at a USC vs. Notre Dame football game.

The ninety minute patriotic extravaganza ends with the participants and the crowd singing a longing, heartfelt folk song, "Arirang" (아리랑). This version, I was told, is about a young wife longing for the return of her husband, who has been away in a war. To both North and South Koreans it symbolizes a longing for the unification of the country into one, once again.

Kaesong area, North Korean soldier at ease.

Kaesong area, North Korea. Tomb of the 14th century Koryo Dynasty king and his Mongolian wife known as the the Hyonjongrung Royal Tomb.

The distorted message we were continuously fed is well illustrated by the Victorious Fatherland Liberation War Museum, which, among other things, had exhibits "proving" the South had invaded the North to start the Korean War. For example, there was a prominently displayed framed letter from John Foster Dulles to Syngman Rhee, the first president of South Korea. The guide giving us the museum lecture said the letter proved that the United States Secretary of State was planning the invasion of the North with Syngman Rhee well before the war began.

I lagged back from the group as it moved on to other "outrages" and studied the letter. It actually was a thank you note from Dulles, who was at the time a New York lawyer, well before he became Secretary of State, thanking Rhee for an autographed book Rhee had sent him. This was their proof!

At our farewell dinner the night before, we were placed, as usual, in a restaurant way out of sight of any other guests, in a separate room. That night there was a Chinese tour group huddled like us, separated from the rest of the restaurant. After about ten minutes one of the Chinese tourists came to our group and offered us some wine. The courtesy was extended back, and pretty soon both groups were merrily mingling. It was as if we both had been so corralled, herded and directed that we had to blow off some steam or we would burst. Surprisingly, the Chinese were as fed up with the propaganda and restrictions as we were. It was great fun.

By the last day of the trip the propaganda outpouring had become quite tiresome, and one tended to "zone out" when it would begin. Our male guide that last bus trip on the last day, just before disembarking for the airport and prior to giving us instructions on what we would do next, addressed us with obvious humor, reciting the complete string of propaganda epithets we had heard throughout the previous four days. It was hilarious, and the bus erupted in cheering and clapping. The team of "watchers" all laughed and clapped along with us.

I'll leave you with this image. On that last bus trip some of our younger fellow-visitors urged our favorite guide to stand up and use the bus microphone to sing a song to us. After much urging, hand clapping and foot stomping, this lovely young woman stood up and started to sing "Arirang." Dead silence in the bus, as she sang slowly and beautifully, with such heartfelt feelings, that tears were not far from us all.

Malaysia

The Datuk* was a smooth operator who wanted us to buy his palm oil plantation so we could get control of the insurance company it held as a subsidiary. No dice.

He also wanted twenty percent of the new company—for no capital contribution—since there was a *Bumi* requirement for foreign companies that required you to cut in locals at no cost to them. We demurred.

I did have fantasies, however, about owning a Malaysian tea plantation. They are very famous. The dream evaporated when I was told by one of the most successful tea plantation owners that the bugs would drive me crazy.

I had visited several plantations in Sri Lanka and Japan, and the visuals were great. Rolling hills of discreet tea bushes made oval by the constant picking of the green leaves. Various shades of green in the sunlight. All very orderly and, like many dreams, quite out of synch with reality.

When you live in Singapore, Malaysia is like your lurking crazy uncle who lives next door. You are never quite sure what they are going to do next.

It is that big country next door that can shut off your water any time, close the Causeways and delay traffic. Through Malaysia was the route the Japanese invaders took. Nevertheless, it has the lure of much cheaper prices and sends lots of workers into Singapore. There is, however, the feeling that the Malaysians just don't like

---

*A traditional Malay honorific title.

the Chinese Singaporeans very much. Why else would they have kicked Singapore out of Malaysia in 1965, just a few years after Singapore had folded into the country and ceased to exist as an independent entity? The TV appearance of Lee Kuan Yew bursting in tears as he told the country they had been kicked out is one of the iconic images all Singaporeans hold in their collective consciousness.

I only journeyed a few times into Malaysia, just to see the sights and try to do some business. One time I drove almost all the way up the East Coast and then came down the West. I also stayed in Malacca once to see the sights, especially where St. Francis Xavier was buried and unburied in his quixotic journey to his final "resting" place in Goa, India, where he is displayed in a glass casket. It's good they didn't try and do a Mao or Ho Chi Minh on him and wax him up. It's bad enough not letting the poor guy rest in peace.

From today's perspective it is difficult to envision Malacca and Goa as very important pivotal settlements in the 1500's, as part of the Portuguese and Jesuits' international expansion. Sleepy towns is what I saw.

Kuala Lumpur, the capital, is glitz and "mine is bigger than yours," as the Petronas Towers were briefly the tallest buildings in the world. Nevertheless, there are many old sections of the city where colonial buildings have been preserved.

Being a Muslim country, headscarves abound and mosques are everywhere. It has always disturbed me that if you are a Chinese in Malaysia you cannot convert to become a Muslim, and that Muslims are forbidden to convert to any other religion. This is true for all Muslim countries, as far as I know.

There are separate schools for non-Muslims, which pretty much means the Chinese population. It is said that one of the motivating factors of kicking Singapore out of Malaysia in 1965 was that with the addition of the large population of Singapore Chinese, the

Malaysia countryside Family watersports.

Malays felt the newcomers would have too much political power. Lee Kuan Yew, at the time of admission, immediately started organizing the People's Action Party (PAP), and this no doubt scared the hell out of the ruling *domos*. Today, there are still limits imposed on the Chinese citizens. There are also limits to the ranks they can achieve in the military and foreign services.

Malaysia is the only place I have heard of that has a handful of kings, with the top dog rotating between nine ruling families over five year terms. Sultans and Rajas are everywhere. As head of state they have no real political power, but have lots of perks and *Ringgits* (money). Also they have to be elected. No, not voted on by the unwashed; only the other kings can vote. Pretty much it seems to follow seniority, but doesn't have to. With all the opulence of

Near Kuala Lumpur, Malaysia.
Open market stall.

their palaces and the adulation of the common man, I wonder if it is as confining as the Japanese or Thai monarchies, which seem to drive the wives, especially in Japan, a bit looney. I imagine it is hard to keep a grip when all around you are bowing and scraping and, indeed, telling you what to do next.

At Ascendant Capital we tried to buy a number of Malaysian insurance companies, but finally gave up when the government official in charge of granting licenses told me in private that he would never approve an American purchaser. I guess I could have claimed we were really a Cayman Island company listed on the Irish Exchange but, no doubt, to no avail.

One thing that you must do while in Malaysia is eat a disgusting *durian*, a Southeast Asian fruit whose inside is considered by some as one of the great delicacies and by others (me) as a little like eating a rotten, slimy slug. Most hotels ban it from their premises because of the pungent odor even before it is sliced. This shows their eminent good sense.

One place that is very special is the island of Langkawi at the very northwestern tip of Malaysia. My dear friends Liz and John Robins from London were regular annual visitors to the Datai resort, and convinced me to try it. Langkawi is known as the "jewel of Kedah" (the Malaysian state) and is one of the many islands in the Andaman Sea close to the mainland. Thailand is just a few miles away. The Datai is a typical tropical resort, with a lovely beach and individual lodges. I relaxed a few days there. You can experience both the beach and jungle.

So there it is, my Malaysia, which turned out to be more enjoying its uniqueness and lounging in my jungle hut than completing any real business ventures.

The Philippines

Entering Manila is entering a traffic jam. The multicolored Jeepneys are an eyeful, and remind me of some of the decorated trucks you see in India. They add to the traffic confusion, but at least they are amusing. I'm told there have been many improvements since the late 90's, when I was last there. Let's hope so, because my visits have been disastrous.

I scheduled a very important board meeting to consider buying a large multinational insurance company; our board member Michael Butt flew in from Bermuda for the meeting. I think it took him three aircraft changes to get there. The actual meeting went fine, but the infrastructure failed. We had several blackouts, which were complete power failures. That ended the PowerPoint presentations. The power failures were intermittent and lasted as long as a half hour, and just when you thought the coast was clear and everything was fixed, it would happen again.

There was also some kind of a labor dispute that became a strike that, in turn, made horrible traffic, impossible traffic. We were not happy. Maybe we should have reflected on Magellan before we decided on this as a venue for a meeting, but one of the reasons was that the company we were interested in had a Philippine unit.

One time I visited to see a variety of local companies, introduced by my friend George SyCip, whose father was a legend in Philippine business. I went to one company after another and met some very courteous CEOs, but never accomplished much.

In trying to acquire a company in the Philippines I even met in Tokyo with ambassador Alfonso Yuchengco, the founder of the

Malayan Insurance Company and paterfamilias of the Yuchengco
Group Companies, one of the largest family-owned conglomerates
in the Philippines. He was very correct and appropriate, and did
not wish to meet me in the embassy itself since it was a matter
involving an investment in his company. I admired his uprightness
in not mixing private business with the nation's business. Later in
the Philippines I met multiple times with his daughter who ran
the insurance company, but to no avail.

One disconcerting aspect of business in Manila was you had to
have a high degree of security if you were a prominent Philippine
business person. When you visited headquarters in the Makati
business district, there were lots of private guards with shotguns.
They would even be stationed inside offices, hanging around the
reception areas with wicked-looking shotguns.

The father of a young family I knew in Singapore headed a
prominent insurance company, and I asked why he was in
Singapore and not Manila. "I'm afraid of being kidnapped." "Who
would do that?" "The police."

There were gangs of policemen who would pull your car over and
then kidnap the passengers. It was strictly a dollars-for-ransom
scheme.

I had kidnap and ransom insurance. When I was active in
Southeast Asia, one aspect of it was that you could never tell
anyone you had coverage. That is, unless you ended up in the
clutches of some very nasty people. I would like to alert all
possible kidnappers that I no longer have the coverage.

One of my London clients was in the kidnap and ransom business.
Very exotic and exciting. I had thought it was about black-clad
ninjas scaling walls and freeing the poor captive. Kidnapping was
an established business, and when some poor executive of
Standard Oil was captured and held for ransom there was a
theoretical menu. Corporate presidents were worth several
million, vice-presidents were about three-quarters of that, lesser

executives even less. They kidnapped; you paid; they released.

The only trouble occurred when the kidnappers were amateurs. That was trouble, because they didn't know the system and, especially, didn't know how to release the captive without either hurting them or getting caught. Most of the kidnap action in those years was in Central and South America. I'm afraid the business has no doubt changed with the Middle Eastern turmoil and dedicated religious zealots.

The Philippines was supposed to be one of those countries that was going to emerge from WWII with both a linguistic advantage, namely English, and a connection to the USA. It hasn't happened yet.

Siem Reap, Cambodia.
Buddha, Angkor Wat.

Cambodia

Before the sun came up I took my bicycle and peddled into the quiet, sealed-off park of Angkor Wat.

I decided that it would be peaceful and give me a good feeling of this amazing place to try to be alone in it. I parked my bike where it looked like it wouldn't be stolen and walked across the causeway entrance into the temple. It was quiet and lovely as, gradually, early streaks of sunlight slid into the passages and open spaces.

I perched on an inside ledge and let the feelings of the place seep in. Pow! Within minutes some guy with a large video camera burst into my area, almost hitting me with his exaggerated lens, dragging along a small group of fellow Scandinavians. So much for tranquility and solitary contemplation in a world heritage site.

No matter how early or late you go, there are always others. Of course, it isn't like midday when these places are overrun and, depending on where you are in the temple, you either have many others, or only a few.

Angkor Wat is one of the hundreds of temples that are strewn all over this area. It appears quite random until you see the overall plan and realize it is very carefully laid out—and the land area is huge. It was established in the early 12th century, and was once the center of the Khmer Empire. It ebbed and flowed over the course of centuries, through wars and religions settling in, which then were deposed by others. It was "lost" to modern western memory until some French archeologists rediscovered it and popularized it for the western world in the 1860's. Ever since then the whole area has been undergoing a gradual revealing of itself

Cambodia village life near Phnom Penh.

apart from tangled vines and choking tree trunks. These latter temples, still in the grip of trees and vines, are also now accessible, and I found them having an impact greater than ones that had been restored.

One of the most photographed Wats is Angkor Thom, with its multiple sculptured faces looking in all directions. Like Shelley's Ozymandias, no doubt these rulers once said "Look on my works, ye Mighty, and despair!"—and they have come to the same end.

The town that is the entrance point for all this is Siem Reap. Someone told me that the local children didn't have many toys and I should bring some in a bag to give it to the hotel concierge to distribute. Fortunately, my guide and his sidekick who picked me up at the airport dissuaded me from doing this, suggested I give them out myself and walked me through an area where there would be lots of kids.

We only had to walk a few blocks off the main thoroughfare to find dirt paths that led to neighborhoods of houses on stilts, with families gathered around the base of these very simply constructed

Angkor, Cambodia. Angkor Thom.

Phnom Penh, Cambodia. The killing fields skulls.

homes made from readily available materials. There were platforms that people sat on at ground level, and often there were a few animals like pigs and chickens rummaging about. When I asked someone why the houses were on stilts since there was no threat of flooding, the answer was clearly stated, "That's where the ghosts come and go."

With my guide doing the talking, we engaged the little groups in conversation—and kids came running. It was really joyful as each one got a unique little toy. We went from family to family and, as these things often do, the kids' "telegraph network" soon had clumps of kids come running.

At one place we came to a swimming hole with a bunch of little boys having a grand time in the water, but soon they gathered around us for their treats. This whole experience was as memorable as the famous temples.

As with all small villages, there was an open market that provided a wide variety of wonderful vegetables but more so an array of locals with weathered visages and unique dress. It was a delight just to wander around.

I also visited Phnom Penh with a group from Singapore that had gotten together to help build some new houses for a small community.

This is a city with a dreadful past, that of the Khmer Rouge, who took over Cambodia in 1975 and pushed almost everyone out and into the countryside. It wasn't like any other transformation when one power supplants another, such as when the Communist armies marched into Shanghai in 1949. No, this was on an inhuman scale of suffering and methodical murder. The very day the Khmer Rouge entered Phnom Penh people were ordered out of their houses and, if they happened to wear glasses, were shot then and there. Why? Because if you wore glasses you were obviously an intellectual and didn't belong in the new agrarian state. There were other killings—university professors and really anyone they arbitrarily suspected might not approve of pushing the society back to the Middle Ages.

On the very day I arrived, a disturbing event occurred. I don't remember what it was, but the government took some fairly innocuous action. It was as if the whole city collectively blinked and stood frozen for a brief second. I asked a local what had occurred and they said, "We thought that it might be starting again." That's how traumatic the years under the Khmer Rouge were.

The horrible heritage of genocide is preserved not only in the deepest, darkest dreams of those who lived through it, but by two very horrifying places: the infamous Tuol Sleng prison, now a genocide museum in Phnom Penh, and the Killing Fields just out of town.

The prison is a multistory, plain building with room after room

Siem Reap, Cambodia. Angkor Wat at sunset.

with displays of the inhumanity that took place there. What is really riveting is inside each doorway as you enter a room is a contemporary photo and biography of a jailer and what despicable things are attributed to him. Then right next to the old prison photo is a new one taken of the same person in recent years and a short identifying paragraph about what he is doing now. It is chilling and fascinating. They know who these people are and where they are. These little photos and descriptions are unusually powerful. They read something like this: "Mr. Moui, who was the main torturer," and then inserted is testimony from one or many who suffered at his hands, "is now a fisherman in such-and-such a village." He is then given a few lines to try to justify his own actions.

Only in recent years has there been a UN tribunal set up in Cambodia to address the crimes of some of the top officials, including the prison warden. The usual defense is, "They made me do it. I would have been killed if I didn't follow orders." Sounds like the Nazi defense. It didn't work then and hopefully it won't work now.

The Killing Fields are a different kind of horror. This is the place where they have exhumed hundreds of the bodies of people who were shot, and the bones and skulls are piled up in a memorial. Although it is a bit macabre, it didn't strike me as powerfully as those little photos in the prison. Maybe because this is a lovely green field surrounded by old trees and sunshine. Little does it reveal of its past without the pile of skulls.

Exploring the city, I took some motorbike taxis, and also got some money from an ATM, where I found it only dispensed US dollars. When I later asked about why didn't I get Cambodian currency the person answered, "Because our currency isn't worth anything."

I had the privilege of spending the afternoon with two Ministers of State, the Women's Minister and the Roads Minister, who were friends of a close friend of mine. They were husband and wife, and members of the government representing the Royal Party, which apparently was all over the place politically and only had limited following despite Cambodia having a king, the famous or infamous Norodom Sihanouk, and, more recently, his son.

We toured around the city, and each time we were on an especially wide and well-done road, the Roads Minister would say, "This was given by the Japanese" or Americans, or some other country. I asked, "Don't you build any roads yourself?" The response: "We have no money." I guess the principal job of the Roads Minister was to get others to build roads.

His very attractive wife had a completely different portfolio, part of which was keeping the US aid agencies happy with their progress in women's rights. She told the story of her battling with a non-governmental organization (NGO) over the closing of a whorehouse, or as the blue-nose insurance rating books identify

The outskirts of Phnom Penh, Cambodia. Newly built and old home.

them, "women's boarding and lodging with transient male guests."

We discussed the whole subject of NGOs and their relationship to the government, and the Women's Minister said, "They are more powerful than we are. They complain to the US embassy and push them to try to get us to do what they see as 'what's right.' Well, what they think is right for the USA isn't always consistent with our practices and heritage. Their power comes from influencing the grants to Cambodia from the US, and if they complain enough the State Department just downgrades us a notch. The consequences are dramatic, as multiple programs are cut off that have not a thing to do with the issue that stimulated the complaint. There is no reasoning with these groups. They have the funds and we don't. I'm having to fly to Washington D.C. to try to move up from being downgraded because, according to them, we didn't act the way they wanted in terms of holding the ladies of

Near Phnom Penh, Cambodian.
Children at home.

the whorehouse in jail. They, of course, yell 'trafficking and corruption' and the State Department just listens to them."

This complaint of nonprofit NGOs causing trouble is one of the reasons China has been reluctant to allow a broad sector of activity for NGOs. Essentially, the bureaucracy sees these extra-governmental organizations as meddlers in activities they have no business in. Most NGOs by their very existence point out and accomplish things that need to be done that aren't being done by the government. Nations that don't have an open society don't like this. Right now a Chinese friend of mine is in the second year of a government project to look at the whole area of NGOs and how to license them while keeping some kind of string attached. There are a few "fast track" experiments going on in Shenzhen and Yunnan, one of the southern provinces.

While there, I made some house-building efforts, which I found really quite exerting. It isn't just taking a hammer and pounding some nails, as it would appear when you see Jimmy Carter helping Habitat for Humanity. Our group from Singapore had about ten members, most with no experience with tools of any kind. Fortunately for us, the local charity was fully experienced in handing "tenderfoots" and left the heavy jobs, such as the basic structural work, to themselves, giving us the more straightforward tasks of putting the floor in place or pounding in the corrugated siding. Each house had been prepared by the local charity, so that really we weren't building a house as much as finishing it off. It took two days to do several homes, and it was very, very hard work. My respect for artisans was forever enhanced.

At the end of our few days there was a gathering of the small community where we had been working. The families whose houses we constructed were officially given the "keys" to their new abodes. Of course, there were no keys as these are open-air homes on stilts without doors or windows. The home is one large room with open window areas cut into the corrugated siding, and a high ceiling. It is made primarily with local materials. Cooking and the "bathroom" were outside in separate structures.

The toilet seemed to be a communal one, and there were little cooking areas, which I assume were allocated to the closest house.

One of the families we presented with their new home burst into tears of joy when it was handed over. It was very touching. Their old place was on the mud ground and had no floor other than the soil. It was dark and small. No wonder they were jubilant in getting a new home.

Shanghai, China.
Fuxing Park.

Shanghai

To "look through my eyes" and see Shanghai as I do, you must first understand that I grew up in a very small city compared to this one. When I was a child in San Francisco it was a small enough place that you went to kindergarten in the same school where your mother, uncles and aunts had gone. My sister and brothers proceeded and followed me there. The children you met there remained acquaintances if not friends, for the rest of your life. You followed each other in your first dancing class at Mr. Kitchen's (a place you couldn't escape, no matter how much you begged your mother not to make you go). You went through your early life, through school, through this progression of dancing lessons and almost into college with many of the same neighborhood kids.

I remember playing in the street as a youngster and having my grandmother drive by. She'd stop and inspect me, then decide my t-shirt was not enough and tell me to put on a sweater. It was as if the city was a neighborhood. My grandfather, whom we called Pa, lived a few doors away in the house where my mother was born. I had aunts, uncles and cousins living within walking distance. As an elementary school student you could take the streetcar or "dinky" cable car (that's what we always called the Clay-Washington line to differentiate it from the much-larger California line) home from school without your mother worrying at all.

It was inevitable that wherever you went someone knew you or your family. Even the police (or cops as we called them) interacted with you. When I was in high school, a group of us decided it would be a grand idea to climb up inside one of the landmark

Shanghai, China, view from my home.

Shanghai, China.
The Bund.

buildings, the Palace of Fine Arts, which was left over from the 1915 Panama-Pacific Exposition. Noted Bay Area architect Bernard Maybeck had designed it in the Grecian style, with Corinthian columns, but it was just a shell, a structure with nothing inside it. It was at that time still made out of its original hardened papier-mâché so if you really tried—as we did—you could plop off big chunks in your hand.

We climbed to the very top and went outside the dome on a thin ledge and pushed a few of the faux Greek urns into the duck pond about ten stories below. There were big splashes and ducks flying, and then, at the exit, a squad car of San Francisco's finest waiting for us. Oh no! There we were, wearing our tell-tale St. Ignatius jackets and caught red handed. What did the cops do? The took our names and said if they ever caught us again they would call our mothers.

Our doors were always unlocked. The ice man came up from the basement and slid his ice into the top half of the ice box. The delivery boy came up the back stairs and left the groceries on the kitchen table. George came on Fridays and set new wood and coal in the fire places and did the heavy cleaning, like washing the front steps. He always sat in his yellow Mercury, parked at the corner and ate lunch by himself. A young black man named Buchanan washed the windows periodically. The names float up through time to me, making up the panoply of life growing up. There were Jack and Lee, Claude and Marie, Van, Mrs. Rutledge the baby nurse and Dr. Gelston the family doctor with his Parker 51 pen and handy long "needle" to lance our ear aches as he sat at our bedside. Lois, a former movie actress turned governess, later a Yellow Cab driver. Mary the Japanese day cleaner. We knew the grocery man, the butcher (Herman), the laundry man (Mr. Bedacaré). Then there was Emma, who cooked for us and "whooped" us if we were bad. She came from the deep south. Her slave father had been freed by Abraham Lincoln's Emancipation Proclamation, or as Emma called it, so aptly, "the day freedom cried out." We learned the smell of collard greens, black-eyed peas and the most wonderful cornbread in the world from her. She carried a straight razor in her purse and said, "no one is going to mess with you kids." We periodically begged her open her purse and show us, the same way we would ask to be shown the gun of the beat cop who came by to collect monthly fee for special watching of the neighborhood. San Francisco was a town in which Emma could buy a house for her large family not 10 blocks from ours. And our family and hers knew each other. Her son, whom we all called Sonny Boy, would come in by the back and sometimes sit in the kitchen. Emma started with our family in the 40's and died with us in the 60's, and in some small ways, we remained intertwined. When my mother died in 1987 I noticed a black man I didn't know at her funeral. It was Sonny Boy, who had read her obituary in the paper and came to pay his respects.

Within such a community, you never knew when someone from the past might resurface, and even come to your aid. Once I was down at the docks giving a speech as a candidate for Congress to the Laborers Union, one of the roughest, toughest bunch of men in the city. Internally, I was quaking in my boots. The audience looked at me like a kid and didn't react at all to my best lines. I finished to modest intermittent applause. As I stood dumbly on the stage, out of the corner of my eye I saw this burley black man rushing toward me. He grabbed me and enveloped me in his huge arms. "This is Rosa's boy," he declared to the throng. He's "our boy. You have to vote for him!" It was our cook Rosa's husband Arthur coming to my rescue. The place erupted in genuine cheering and applause. Arthur was their "brother" in labor and his endorsement meant something. If Arthur said it, they would do it.

Of course, in this heavily Asian-influenced city that I grew up in, there were Japanese and Chinese around us. My mother hired Japanese women to do light house keeping. A Chinese couple that worked for us gave me a little sheep dog named Bushki, who responded only to commands in Chinese, since they had raised him.

I didn't just hear the languages, I had to use Chinese to get my dog to sit. So maybe it's not so surprising that I now live in Shanghai, the world's largest city proper. But how different it looks from my original home.

□□ □□ □□
□□ □□ □□

I live in a very modern complex of fourteen twenty-four-story towers housing about 1,000 residents, mostly Chinese. This residential area is probably greater than all the apartments on San Francisco's Russian Hill put together. At the main entrance gate the ever-present cabs are lined up waiting for customers as people filter out. Each cab company has their own colors (white, pale blue, maroon, gold, dark blue, red) and there are various opinions and stories about which color cab is best. I don't see much differ-

Praying at Shanghai Confucian Temple.

ence except in the special cabs that were used at Expo (Shanghai's version of a world's fair, held in 2012) because the drivers who got those cabs were the most experienced and knowledgable. You can tell by their identity card displayed in the the cab which in addition to a photo and number shows stars for duration and quality of service. It is rare to get one with more than one or two stars, but most normal cab drivers have none. The most I've seen is six in an Expo driver's cab although five is supposed to be the maximum.

I have absorbed my own map of Shanghai in my head and know certain routes for my cab home or walking from place to place. Shanghai is mostly flat so walking is quite enjoyable. There are many nooks and crannies to be explored on almost every block. After my morning coffee, breakfast and run through the stories on the web and overnight emails, I head to the gym. I try to be there at seven, but don't always make it. If I'm not in the gym, at about 8:10 am each weekday morning I hear the loudspeaker from the children's school across the street—the principal starting her morning homily to the students. This is followed by a loud playing of the National Anthem, which can be quite stirring in its march cadence.* Sometimes the song isn't sung with the proper gusto so the principal makes the children sing it again.

There is a cultural "jet lag" from the older generation to this. No easily recalled memories of the hard past to lay out before this young group entering the stream of life. In Shanghai we are all trying to find our path, young and old, newcomer, generational resident. Everything is in flux here but maybe not more so than any of a handful of dynamic cities across the world. Still, old fashioned and contemporary are locked hand in hand. Family,

---

*March of the Volunteers 义勇军进行曲 Yìyǒngjūn Jìnxíngqǔ. Arise! All those who don't want to be slaves! Let our flesh and blood forge our new Great Wall. As the Chinese people have arrived at their most perilous time. Every person is forced to expel his very last cry. Arise! Arise! Arise! Our million hearts beating as one, Brave the enemy's fire, March on! Brave the enemy's fire, March on! March on! March on! On!

Confucianism, the CCP, social media blocked and unblocked, chic and pitiful, and business always business, money always money, the city revolves around all these things.

Very early each day the blue clad janitorial crews begin their morning clean up of the front porches and push their large garbage bins to a central garbage collection point. Several tenants walking their dogs pass by. Birds are jumping around the flower beds and the grass, pecking at crumbs and chirping as they go.

As I head out onto my street I get the wonderful experience of observing the ease people seem have with their surroundings which almost step-by-step juxtaposes the old and new. Cars stream out of the underground garage and guards open and shut the gates, salute you as you leave, and stop visitors on their way in if they don't know them. Bicycles, motor scooters, grannies pushing baby strollers and dog walkers are all part of the morning exodus.

Across the street is a very contemporary Thai restaurant next door to them has an unidentified double door entrance which the

Shanghai, China.

Shanghai, China, National Day.

Shanghai, China, light snowfall.

Wujiang City, China.
Hotel aquarium.

maître d' at the Thai restaurant says is a "place you don't want to go" (which means a massage parlor that isn't). There's a newsstand and the school. Moving down the block are a variety of "hole in the wall" stores that have very helpful and necessary services, including a stationery store/printer, game store, soft goods, cookies and a 24-hour market. I think the last may double as a part-time police station because there always seem to be police motorbikes parked in front and cigarette-smoking policemen in the back room.

At the corner a new residential building called Shanghai One has opened in the past year and the façade shows that it is mostly a new Kempinski hotel. I am a constant visitor since you can get to my gym through their lobby. There is also a street entrance for the gym down the block where most people go in. I would expect the Kempinski would get a bit irritated if the gym users all used their lobby to enter but I feel pretty comfortable not only because I use

Zhao Zhuang Village, China. Her first crayons ever.

the dining room fairly often but also having gotten to know their manager Ms. Karina Ansos, a good German (like the hotel).

It has been interesting watching the hotel struggle in its opening phases through the variations in the dining room staff and management. I got a receptionist from my former gym a job when they opened and the then manager promised she could learn the system and then move into managing the dining area which serves breakfast, lunch afternoon tea, and dinner. After about one week her new boss was fired and she was made a waitress. She quit. The next manager lasted about a month and was fired as well. The interesting aspect about him was that he told me the day before he was fired that he had just proposed to his girlfriend in that very restaurant. Poor guy now has no job.

The Shanghai Oriental Notary Public Office is on the opposite corner. Turning from Datian Lu into Fengyang Lu is a natural foods market, two ad hoc hot food sellers and a few stands for breakfast rolls and patties, dress shops, a "gambling den" open to the street that seems to be mostly Go and card players at very elementary card tables. Next comes the barber, haircuts ¥20 (USD $3) pretty good, all scissors. Then comes another soft goods store, a real estate office, another dress shop and another office of the Shanghai Oriental Notary Public.

Every week day a husband and wife team roll out a portable burner and wok with its attached umbrella to cover them and their street visitors. A little dog sleeps at their side, the wife kneading dough and breaking it into palm sized pieces, pressing it flat; the husband with tongs moves it into the wok conducting with this long pincers with baton-like movements, shifting slowly baking thin biscuits, which after a while are moved with precision to a hot plate and stacked up, awaiting the flow of customers. The couple leaves in the early evening.

The spot across the street is filled at night by a noodle and vegetable hot dinner seller with his portable wok and trickle of late night clubbers and late night construction workers. On that side of the street are high rise buildings including the Kempinski Hotel, a tall office building under construction, and another tall office building with a car dealer, Citibank office and the ubiquitous Starbucks.

As you stroll along the street you may see a lady pushing a wheelchair with the person in the chair completely covered with a blanket, like a mobile ghost, while the local key maker puts out an advertisement and a chair on the sidewalk to lounge in. Or there might be men pedaling flatbeds designed cycles with three wheels, equipped with bells they ring constantly to let you know they are there and will collect items from you.

In Shanghai, you know you belong when you meet someone on the street whom you know, which for me isn't very often. On the other hand why do I (and others) not make eye contact with other

Caucasians when we pass in the street? Is it because we want to be the only outsider here?

□□ □□ □□
□□ □□ □□

There is a new Metro station going up in Jing'an Sculpture Park next to the new Natural History Museum in what the architects call a nautilus shape, meaning sea shell, that is close to being finished. The scaffolding is beginning to be removed and the building is emerging in what looks like an innovative design. However I don't know what to make of the façade, with its "squiggly crack lines." The concept was fresh a few years ago but now seems a bit trite. Maybe the time lapse from conception to realization has transformed something unique into something less so but I best wait until the whole presentation is unveiled. China continuously surprises so I'll give them the benefit of the doubt and see what the final transformation is.

New construction is ever present in Shanghai and going on in almost every block both here in Puxi and in Pudong. The newly opened Museum of Modern Art in the iconic China Expo Pavilion and the Power Station of Art, a contemporary art museum, are just a few of the civic related projects just completed.

The little shops along my streets are gradually going "up market" with occasional refurbishing of what are basically concrete box spaces with hanging florescent lights. Not many years ago these same places didn't even have fronts, just open spaces with goods stacked up. You can still see a lot of this down Beijing Xi Lu towards the Bund where various trades dominate each block with plumbing shops all along one side and the next block electrical shops, or siding sellers and so on.

If you step across the street from these shops you can see they are pop up additions off the fronts of the apartment blocks. This is especially noticeable on Fengxian Lu where the tree canopied streets line the blocks outside ornate buildings with exotic statues on the façade. They are now aesthetically ruined by the carbuncles of additions, boxlike stores poking out the front of each building. Along Beijing Xi Lu in my neighborhood, the city has recently removed long blocks of shops and put in small green areas so the buildings behind are now exposed and redone to show their fin de siècle façades.

Of course the neighborhood streets are not empty. There are people of all classes and states of dress mingled together walking down the street to work, coming or going from construction sites, taking the air in ones pajamas, and lining up to buy a breakfast items. Many emerge from the buildings behind the shops that are sort of 1920's buildings with lanes and alleys but not quite the old Shikumen;* these are interspersed with taller old apartment blocks. It is inevitable that these will be knocked down and replaced by gleaming towers like the ones that are already in the neighborhood.

Sweepers are on the job early and seem to be ever present, keeping things tidy. They are needed and despite refuse boxes, almost every block people still blithely discard wrappers, plastic bottles and anything else they want to get rid of by throwing it on the sidewalk. However there are many street cleaners who are quite diligent at sweeping up. They are joined from time to time by mini street cleaning mobile machines that spray water in the cleaned out trash bins and spots on the curb. These wagons are followed later by those large water spraying, spinning broom machines found in most urban cities. It is a constant effort. This is a big change from years ago when public cleanliness was not a priority.

---

*Shikumen (stone gate) houses are two or three-story townhouses with the front yard protected by a high brick wall. Each residence is connected and arranged in straight alleys, known as a lòng-tang (弄堂). The entrance to each alley is usually surmounted by a stylistic stone arch. The whole resembles terrace houses or townhouses commonly seen in Anglo-American countries, but distinguished by the tall, heavy brick wall in front of each house. The literal meaning "stone gate" refers to the strong gateway to each house. —Wiki

Heng Shan, China. Restaurant in Jiangsu province which adjoins Shanghai.

There is often still something to be desired in the public lavatories although they are light years ahead of what they used to be. And when it comes to graffiti? I think I've seen one rather hasty scrawl, and it was painted over immediately. Taggers couldn't do their damage in the day time, because there is no such thing as an empty street. If they came in the dead of night, it would be painted over the next morning. The upshot is, it's simply not worth doing. Not only risky, but futile.

There are several other city workers you encounter walking down the street. The most interesting is the Traffic Assistant as his baseball cap exclaims. He wears his blue official outfit and is found on every block where there are parking meters. He always has a white van with sliding doors parked somewhere in the vicinity which inside contains a makeshift office with his gathered papers, tea bottle and an easy chair. When not taking a break he sits curbside in a straight wooden chair and surveys his one-block territory. His target is motorists who want to park. As soon as they begin to park he is on the scene determining how long they will be staying. He then goes to the one parking meter vending machine found in the middle of the block, pushes a button and takes the extruded paper to the waiting driver. Now you may ask why the driver can't walk up to the machine themselves and tap in their time and get a ticket, but no need. This is a country that has to provide jobs for as many of its citizens as possible.

There are several other useful folks as part of the civic corps of helpers. These people help you cross busy intersections. There are brown-clad whistle-blowing traffic "policemen" who aren't policemen, hence they are totally ignored by errant impatient pedestrians. Their only weapon is shame, and they yell or blow a whistle at the person who may or may not then comply. Each corner where these city servants work has a large umbrella he or she can stand under, which also provides a nice shady spot for girls who don't want to get the sun while they wait for the light to change.

At the peak of the rush hour in the morning the street crossing

Nantong, China. Lang Shan, Guangjiao Temple elder.

policemen have an assistant. This person has only a designated jacket with "assistant traffic guide" or something like that. They hold a very small red hand flag and point it in the direction the green signal shows you are free to cross. Almost all of these assistants appear to be either Downs syndrome affected or with limited mental skills. It is disturbing and touching to see them diligently pointing their flags as the signals change.

Once you travel the two long blocks down Fengyang you hit the famous Nanjing Xi Lu, one of the most glitzy shopping streets in Shanghai. From then on for about a mile it is almost all tall modern buildings and international brand stores just as you would see on the world's biggest shopping avenues like Fifth Avenue, Bond Street or the Ginza, all of whom mimic each other. Fortunately there are a few last century apartment buildings with their distinct gentle curved façades still on a few corners. Hopefully they will anchor their corners at least for a while.

Close by there is the Line 2 Metro station. There is a constant flow

Nanjing, China.
Railroad station.

Shanghai, China. Jing'An Sculpture Park.

of people in and out of the entrance which is flanked by the GAP and M&S with large ads as you head for the stairs. Down the stairs you will always find vendors selling jewelry or scarfs and a guy who cleans and puts plastic covers on your mobile phone. Some times there is a lone one-string Erhu player hoping for some coins. If rain is threatened, out of nowhere the umbrella salesmen will materialize with a broad display of wares and be quite willing to quote outrageous prices to westerners until you express a more savvy price and he will immediately come down. There are always lots of food outlets in the passages to the Metro, often a McDonalds.

Once in the station you may have a few more stands selling magazines or candy and then the entrance itself, which has an airport baggage scanning devise for those with large bundles. This was initiated pre–Expo 2010 and has continued. The buzz buzz is that the company that has the scanning contract here, at all the airports and other sites in China, was run by Hu Haifeng 胡海峰, the son of former President of China Hu Jintao. When he became the president of Nuctech, a Tsinghua University–owned company, it was granted a near-monopoly by the central authorities and now accounts for about 90% of the domestic market. Haifeng has now stepped down probably because the company is under multiple corruption and unfair competition claims from overseas.

My experience on the Metro has been really positive. There are eleven active lines with two more to come shortly and nine more announced. They are clean, efficient, arrive very regularly and although pretty packed all the time, in my area I usually find a seat within one or two stops. It is quite efficient for getting around especially when heading for Pudong and the symphony during rush hour, when the tunnels can be quite congested. I have two modest caveats. Sometimes the walk between connecting lines is quite long and even in one case you leave the station building and cross the street to an elevated line, and secondly they stop running too early and not universally on all lines or even stations. Usually it is pretty much down by 11 pm just when the taxis kick up their meter rates.

Back outside, those who stroll down the streets are of course a mixture of everything and everybody you see in cosmopolitan cities from stunningly attractive Chinese women, western tourists, shop girls, to the occasional ragged beggar lying on the sidewalk in various grotesque postures.

Panhandling is not practiced by many but beggars are occasionally found outside a popular tourist destination, restaurant or bar. It appears there is some kind of territorial courtesy because you see the same beggars often at the same place. You also quite often see people scavenging in the trash bins. Not to worry; they apparently make a pretty good living at this.

A man who runs a nonprofit for indigents told me that there is a hierarchy among the street trash bin scavengers with territory and

Shanghai, China. Dance lesson.

routes all sorted out. It is apparently quite lucrative for them within this context. To get these people to adopt another lifestyle is a challenge for this nonprofit because they are used to a certain level of income not immediately available for entry jobs. They are also reluctant to give up the outdoors.

Another group of people you see on shopping streets are the bicycle vendors. Theres are the folks who have flatbed carts attached to their bicycles and park them on the widest sidewalks all the while keeping an eye out for the police. The police will ticket them and I'm told sometimes actually confiscate their little portable store. Of course the merchants who pay huge rents to have their shops on Nanjing Xi Lu or Huaihai Road hate them.

It is quite humorous to see one as they spot a plainclothes policeman and like a flock of wild geese, flee the scene, furiously peddling their bikes only to return minutes later or on an adjacent street. Most of them sell cheap purses, scarves, umbrellas and ripped-off copies of bestsellers.

Always within the group there is one who sells pirate music or movie DVD's (¥5/$0.79) or music CD's. To advertise their wares they constantly play the same Mexican love song "¿Quién será?" It took great effort to find out the name of this song as none of the vendors ever seemed to know despite playing it day and night. I tried Google, Yahoo, everything I could but never could find what it was. I even got a copy and thought the label would tell me, but the street version has no title. Quite by chance I mentioned it to Vivian Li, who knew of an Apple download called SoundHound that identifies the name of songs by listening as it is played. I downloaded it moved my iPhone next to the player and put on my CD. Instantly it identified it. A real marvel of technology. The only exception to everyone playing this song is a vendor outside the magnificent Shanghai Oriental Art Center in Pudong who plays "Starry, Starry Night (Vincent)" over and over, so that you hear it as you enter and leave the hall.

Walking along the streets you pass the motorcycle "taxis" illegal transport found at many central subway exits. They are for very local trips. I've used them once in a while and first you bargain, walk away, bargain, stick to your price (about 1/2 the paltry taxi flag down of ¥14/$2.20) and off you go holding on for dear life.

So it is easy to see this part of Shanghai, Jing'An, has a lot of variety, from the Bentley auto display room to street peddlers and beggars, the high end restaurants and boutiques, to hole-in-the-wall ladies fashions. It's all here right before your eyes and ears, and in the distance you hear "¿Quién será? ¿Quién será?" The theme of Expo 2012 was "Better City – Better Life" and signifies Shanghai's new status in the 21st century as the "next great world city." What could be better?

Final Impressions

While you are living it, you don't think of your various experiences as especially notable. They may generate a story right afterwards to your friends or colleagues, but then you are on to the next thing. The impression may have been made, but only upon later reflection does the seriousness, levity or impact come to you. Writing my reflections has done that for me and hopefully for you, the reader. Maybe it will ever so slightly make us a bit more understanding, generous or open-minded. Let's hope so.

Russell R. Miller is a native of San Francisco, California, and has been working on projects in Asia for almost thirty years. With headquarter offices in Hong Kong and Singapore, he directed two investment funds and in 2002 founded The Spirit of Enterprise, a nonprofit, cultural, educational organization dedicated to fostering the entrepreneurial spirit. Recently, he joined with others to start ZenPlay, a nonprofit aiming to help children's charities.

He also worked for three years in the U.S. Congress in Washington, D.C., and won a contested nomination for a U.S. Congressional seat, although he lost the general election. His papers for that period are found in the Bancroft Library at the University of California, Berkeley, a principal repository library for California History.

Prior to living in Singapore and now in Shanghai, he was an investment banker, having created a specialty firm in the United States that focused on the domestic and international insurance industry. He founded the National Insurance Leadership Symposium, a leadership forum for insurance executives. He served as a trustee and executive committee member of the College of Insurance, St. John's University, in New York. He was a co-founder of the Insurance Industry Charitable Fund.

A recipient of The Republic of Singapore's Pingat Bakti Masyarakat Public Service Medal, he lives in both Shanghai and San Francisco.

Additional copies of this paperback edition of
Snapshots: A Brief Stroll Through Asia may be ordered from Amazon.com

Made in the USA
Charleston, SC
22 December 2013